Shrapnel and Whizzbangs
A Tommy in the Trenches 1914–18

SHRAPNEL AND WHIZZBANGS

A Tommy in the Trenches 1914–18

by

JEREMY MITCHELL

The Memoir Club

First published in 2008 by
The Memoir Club
Arya House
Langley Park
Durham
DH7 9XE

British Library Cataloguing in
Publication Data.
A catalogue record for this book
is available from the
British Library

ISBN: 978-1-84104-192-6

Typeset by TW Typesetting, Plymouth, Devon
Printed by The Cromwell Press Ltd, Trowbridge, Wilts

Dedication

For the grandchildren of George Oswald Mitchell and Josephine Garner – Brian, Laurence, Veronica, Dominic and Alcuin and all who follow them

Contents

List of Illustrations

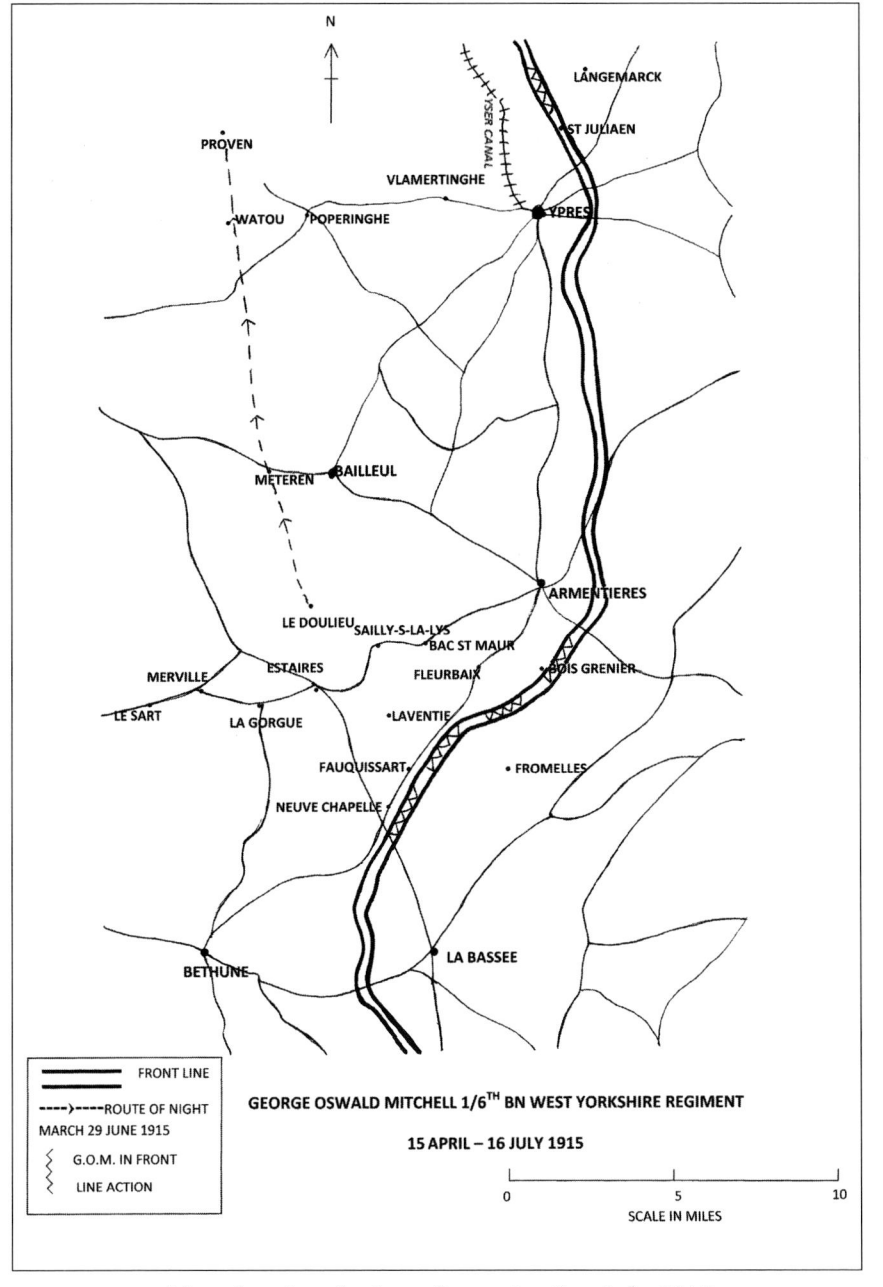

Map showing the front line – April to July 1915

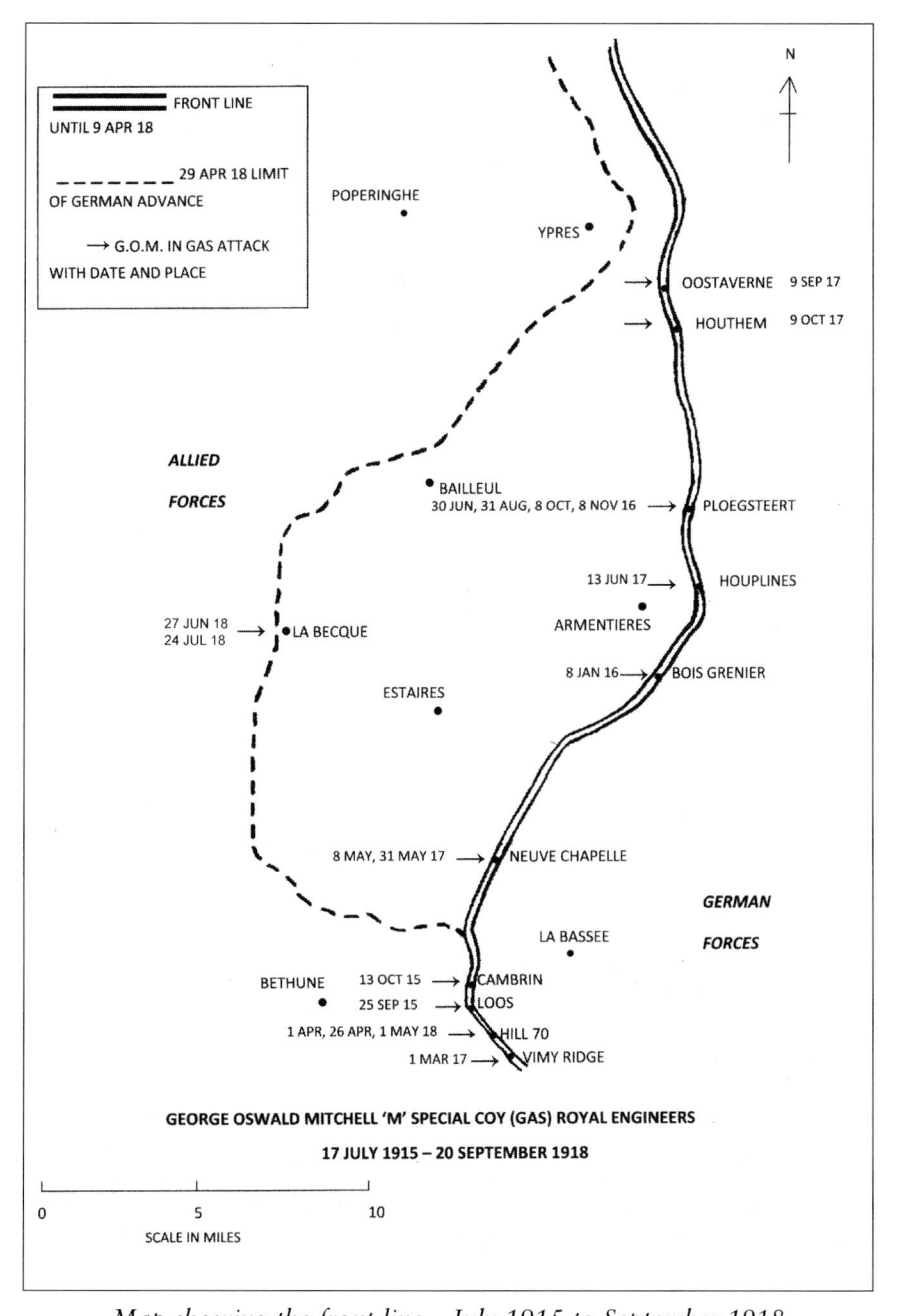

Map showing the front line – July 1915 to September 1918

CHAPTER 1

The Shadow of the Great War

THE BATTLE WAS GOING BADLY FOR ME. On the left flank, the Cameron Highlanders had failed in their rushed attempt to capture the enemy's machine-gun post. The fully automatic Maxim gun had sprayed its destruction through a wide arc from the moment they emerged above the parapet. The piper in his glengarry had been the first to be sent spinning, followed rapidly by the kilted, kneeling riflemen. Their white helmets and red jackets made them absurdly conspicuous, relics from another age, another war. Only those firing from a lying position had escaped the hail of fire to withdraw to the relative safety of the forward trench, where they were then immediately engaged in fending off a German counterattack.

On the right flank, a Royal Artillery mountain gun team had suffered heavy losses in only just surviving an assault by a squadron of mounted Uhlans, galloping towards the British lines with levelled lances. The gun's arrival at the front had been delayed by the slow gait of the mules, more accustomed to the rocky defiles of India's North-West frontier with Afghanistan than the Flanders plain. The barrel, mounting and wheels had been assembled in haste just before the attack started and the German cavalry had been almost on top of the gun before it was able to fire. The gunners had only been saved by a detachment of French North African Zouaves in turbaned fez and baggy trousers, charging at the double with fixed bayonets.

In the centre, confusion reigned. A thin red line of the Worcesters had taken heavy casualties under persistent shelling from two German howitzers. Along the communication trench leading to a small Red Cross tent, two stretcher-bearers with ramrod stiff arms and in perfect step transported a neatly bandaged khaki-clad figure. Two nurses wearing red capes and white aprons over grey ankle length dresses walked alongside, seemingly immune from the bombardment, an oasis of serenity in the surrounding carnage.

I brought up all available reserves to the front to face the expected German assault. A detachment of the Sudanese Camel Corps, recently arrived, was picking its way forward from the rear with some difficulty. The Sudanese riders with their shiny new uniforms were

silhouetted high above the green and brown plain, increasingly vulnerable to enemy fire as they approached the front line. Riflemen of the King's Royal Rifle Corps in their dark green uniforms were running forward, rifles at the trail. However, my Machine Gun Section had gone missing and was nowhere to be found – had it been surreptitiously captured by the Huns? The six Vickers machine guns were capable of holding up a whole enemy brigade. Their absence might be critical.

At this moment, a German howitzer shell scored a direct hit, dislodging the copy of Kennedy's Latin Primer that was supporting the front parapet and knocking over several of the Worcesters. It looked as if all would be lost when, suddenly, the enemy ceased firing. Field Marshall Paul von Benechendorf und Hindenburg, in the person of Robertson, G, came forward offering a truce. The form master had told him that – a rare treat – there would be strawberry jam for tea. As there was an algebra lesson immediately afterwards, it looked as if this battle might never be concluded. Robertson, G. and I packed our soldiers away in their boxes. Next time, we would change sides, and I would command the German army.

*   *   *

I grew up in the shadow of the First World War – 'The Great War' as it was known at the time, the war to end all wars. The Western Front dominated my childhood in the 1930s. Mons, the Marne, Aubers Ridge, Neuve Chapelle, First Ypres, Second Ypres, Thiepval, Cambrai, 'Plug Street' (Ploegsteert), Vimy Ridge, Passchendaele, Loos, the Somme . . . I cannot recall a time when I did not know the familiar litany of battle names. It was almost as if I had myself experienced life in the trenches: the cold, damp dugout, stewed tea and bully beef, 'stand to' at first light, the dawn artillery bombardment, over the top at the blast of the sergeant's whistle and into a storm of bullets. I played out the four years of trench warfare with my collection of model lead soldiers in endless floor battles – against my class mates at my boarding prep school, left hand against right hand in my bedroom alone at home in the holidays.

It wasn't that my father, G.O.M. (George Oswald Mitchell[1]), talked incessantly about his years in the trenches. In fact, he didn't talk about the war much at all, and certainly not about its horrors.

---

[1] My father used his initials partly as an ironic reference to W E Gladstone, four times Liberal Prime Minister during the later part of the nineteenth century: his nickname was G.O.M. – Grand Old Man.

The jokes and stories, though, often came out for an airing. There was the Irish platoon sergeant in their company who played cards all the time. Returning to their dugout from a night patrol in no man's land, after crawling through the mud with blackened faces from shell hole to shell hole and cutting their way through barbed wire entanglements, G.O.M. and his comrades would be met with the words 'And who's for a game of cards now?'

Many of the jokes and stories were part of the foot-slogging soldier's traditional safety valve, subversion of authority – like the two old sweats in a pub, discussing an acquaintance: 'Oh aye, he fought in t'Great War alreet, did Bill, but t'were mostly against t'officers and NCOs, like.' A true story involved a mate from G.O.M.'s company who had stayed in the army after the end of the war to volunteer for the British anti-Bolshevik expedition to northern Russia. The volunteers were given an extra Arctic pay allowance. However, G.O.M.'s friend, who had something of a reputation as a barrack room lawyer, was a keen student of King's Regulations, the bible of army administration. He discovered that soldiers posted east of Suez were entitled to receive an additional Tropical pay allowance. They were indeed east of Suez and, to the adjutant's fury, had to be paid both Arctic and Tropical allowances.

Then there were the sayings, to be repeated at home whenever there was an appropriate occasion: 'Stand back the Buffs – let the West Yorks come through'. Needless to say, the West Yorks were his own regiment, the Buffs a scorned rival from Kent. Sometimes it seemed as if the war was more of a league competition among the British regiments than war to the death with Germany:

> . . . and when we get to Berlin
> the Kaiser he will say
> 'Hoch! Hoch! mein Gott
> vot a cholly fine lot
> ze Vest Yorkshire infantry'.

Not all the badinage of the trenches was complimentary. The RAMC – Royal Army Medical Corps – were libelled as 'Rob All My Comrades' from their alleged practice of rifling the pockets and stealing the watches of dead soldiers as they carried the corpses off the battlefield.

The songs, too, persisted. Many of them had been sung on the march – and there had been a great deal of marching in the First World War, when motorised transport was unknown at the beginning

of hostilities and still something of a luxury at the end. The most famous and enduring was 'It's a long way to Tipperary, it's a long way to go', but there were also 'Carry me back to dear old Blighty', 'Pack up your troubles in your old kitbag and smile, smile, smile', as well as many others. Some were stoical to the point of cynicism – 'Left, left, I had a good job and I left', 'We're here because we're here, because we're here, because we're here', 'We'd be far better off in a home'. One of the more mildly scabrous ones that seems to have disappeared from public memory is worth quoting, as remembered by my sister Joy more than eighty years later:

> If the sergeant drinks your rum, never mind
> If the sergeant drinks your rum, never mind
> He's entitled to a tot
> But he's drunk the bloody lot
> If he's a drunken sot
> Never mind.

Other songs were explicit about the wretchedness and fear that dominated life in the trenches:

> Sing me to sleep where bullets fall.
> Let me forget the war and all.
> I've got the wind up, that's what they say,
> God strafe 'em like hell – till break of day,
> I feel so weary, warworn and sad,
> I don't like this war – it makes me feel bad.
> Dark is my dugout – cold are my feet –
> Waiting for Boches to put me to sleep.

One of these songs articulating weariness with war struck such a chord with my father that he wrote down the words in the war diary that he kept in the trenches:

> I want to go home
> I want to go home
> Shrapnel and whizzbangs
> Around me do roam.
> I don't want to go
> To the trenches no more
> Take me over the sea
> Where the Germans
> Cannot get me
> Thirsty, I don't want to die
> I want to go home.

In another vein, there were the openly sentimental, trench ballads, often – in the days before radio and television – brought back from West End shows to the front line by those returning from leave: 'There's a Long, Long Trail A-Winding', 'Roses of Picardy' and 'Goodbye-ee'. These were for the long, tedious hours in the dugout rather than for the route march.

In the 1920s and 1930s, the 78 rpm records of these and a host of other First World War songs were played on the wind-up gramophone in our suburban living room. Perhaps the one that was played most frequently was George Robey and Violet Lorraine's 'If You Were the Only Girl in the World'. I can remember seeing my mother and father stealing fond glances at each other as the gramophone turntable rumbled round. Of course, all these songs didn't take root just in our family. They became an integral part of the nation's consciousness. In the late 1940s, when I was a conscripted National Service recruit, a private in the Northumberland Fusiliers, my mates and I sang the very same songs – though more often in the back of a three-ton truck than on the march. Later still, many of the songs became part of the bitter canon of remembrance of 1914 to 1918 in Joan Littlewood's fiercely evocative play and film *Oh What a Lovely War*. For my eldest son Laurence, two generations down the line, *Oh What a Lovely War* **was** the First World War.

Then there was the physical detritus of trench warfare that had washed up in our suburban Manchester home. The pliers in the tool box, that had been used for cutting through the enemy's barbed wire. The brass shell case that sat on the living room hearth, housing the poker and fire tongs. A German hussar's ornate cap badge, taken from a prisoner of war, inscribed '*Mitt Gott für König und Vaterland*' (With God for King and Fatherland): it puzzled me – surely God had been on our side, hadn't he? A tattered, yellowing copy of *Canada in Khaki*, a trench publication like the *Wipers* [Ypres] *Times*, full of cartoons, jokes and stories. It is well over sixty years since I last saw it, but my memory conjures up photographic images of some of the pages: a drawing of a Flanders church almost destroyed by shells, with two dogs scavenging in the ruins, and underneath a bitter pastiche of a Burns poem, starting – 'Ye blastit curs/Hae ye nae grace/To caper i' the sacred place?'; a cartoon of a soldier having his hair cut by a comrade, with a ramrod-stiff sergeant standing by:

Sergeant: 'What do you think you're doing having a haircut when you're on duty?'

Soldier: 'It grew while I was on duty, Sarge.'
Sergeant: 'It didn't *orl* grow while you were on duty, did it?'
Soldier: 'Well, Sarge, I'm not having it *orl* cut off, am I?'

Why should I remember this excruciating joke, word for word?

In the 1930s, the literature of the First World War was still relatively meagre. The huge explosion in the number of histories, memoirs and fiction didn't come until much later. However, on the family bookshelves at home there was space for *The History of the Great European War*, published from 1914 onwards in six volumes, appropriately bound in blood red cloth, with gilt lettering and black decorations (I still have the first volume, which, though undated, seems to have been published just after the war started, but the others have drifted away over the years). This 'history' sets out to justify a victorious war and makes little pretence at objectivity. Everyone on the allied side is heroic and virtuous. A photograph of moustachioed Serbian cavalry on parade is captioned 'The Serbians are by no means the cut-throat barbarians they are commonly conceived to be: they have fine soldierly qualities – many of them are cultured and accomplished to a degree.' The French Commander-in-Chief, General Joffre, is lauded as '. . . a man of strong and inflexible will, with a genius for organisation.'

By contrast, the enemy are mean and villainous. A few pages further on, a photograph of the town of Visé with some German soldiers wandering desultorily about is subtitled 'This Belgian town was the first to suffer from the mailed fist: German troops are seen searching the ruined buildings in the expectation of loot.' Even the German philosopher Nietzsche is assigned a role in this moral degradation, described as:

> the expounder of the revolutionary theory that all moral laws are but a remnant of Christian superstition cherishing the virtues of the weak. His ideal, the overman [sic], is to be developed by giving unbridled freedom to the struggle for existence – will seek only his own power and pleasure and knows nothing of pity. Prussian militarism is the modern expression of this ruthless philosophy.

However, it is made clear that Nietzsche got his just deserts – 'He died insane.'

Harmsworth's Universal Encyclopaedia, dating from the early 1930s and nestling in its own bookcase, was full of war-focused entries, with photographs, maps and narrative accounts of the major battles and campaigns. It did not indulge in the crude propaganda of

the *History*, but nevertheless the same moral message came across strongly. The war had not just been about power politics or the defence of Britain's interests. It had been a crusade of good against evil – and good had triumphed.

The same message permeated the fiction I read. I graduated sharply from Hans Andersen's haunting stories (*The Emperor's New Clothes* was my favourite) and the Grimm Brothers' fairy tales to rattling yarns about young Britons doing heroic deeds. On the shelves of my prep school library was a row of nineteenth-century novels by G A Henty, with titles like *Winning His Spurs*, *Under Drake's Flag*, *With Moore at Corunna*, *With Wolfe at Quebec*, *With Kitchener in the Sudan*. However, by the 1930s and 1940s, these empire-building stories had already lost their appeal to modern boys like us. We thought they belonged to a previous generation. More exciting for my friends and me were the W E Johns adventure stories of the fighter pilot Biggles and his chums Algy and Ginger, and the exploits of Bulldog Drummond, written by 'Sapper' (H C McNeile). But far away the most popular were the novels of Percy F Westerman – *Cadet Alan Carr*, *Midshipman Raxworthy*, *When the Allies Swept the Seas*, *The Secret Battleplan* and many more. These portrayed a clean-limbed, clear-eyed young Briton – the hero was always male – finding himself in a position of great danger and eventually triumphing against the (invariably German) enemy. This was the fictional literature of my early childhood. My role model was clearly delineated for me.

All around me were real life role models, though they seemed strangely reluctant to talk about the heroic deeds I thought they must have performed. As well as G.O.M., there were the uncles. Real uncles were thin on the ground. Uncle Rupert, my father's younger brother, had joined up with G.O.M. on the outbreak of the First World War and, like him, had served for four years in the trenches. He must have lied about his age when enlisting, as he was under 17 when war broke out. After the war, Uncle Rupert went on to live a quiet life in his native Yorkshire, working as an income tax clerk. The only time my sister Joy and I ever heard him talk about the war was the last time we saw him, in hospital shortly before he died. He told us how once, on sentry duty behind the front line, he had seen Field Marshal Sir Douglas Haig on horseback, surrounded by a cohort of gold-braided staff officers. Overcome with fury at the loss of life for which he held the British Commander-in-Chief responsible, Uncle Rupert raised his rifle and got Haig in his sights, intending to fire.

Then his nerve failed him and he lowered his gun. That was Uncle Rupert's first and last silent, unwitnessed protest against the carnage of war. It had remained a secret until he told us, sixty years later. His recollection of it was the only occasion on which my sister and I ever saw him display any emotion.

The other real uncle who figured in the family's war history was my mother's brother Jack. He was the uncle I never knew – Corporal John T Garner, of the Queen's West Surrey regiment, killed in battle at Givenchy on 12 February 1916, thirteen years before I was born. All that survives of him is a poem he wrote to my mother on her 15th birthday, carefully preserved in her autograph album, a studio photograph of him in uniform and an *In Memoriam* card.

My mother had another brother, Jim, but, unlike Uncle Jack, his name never surfaced fully in family conversation. It seemed that he had left Bradford to live in London – and therefore, through Yorkshire eyes, had inevitably gone to the bad. A handful of photographs of him survive. He is alone in all of them and they are all posed portraits. In one of them he is wearing a circular brass lapel badge. Bearing the words 'On War Service', this was worn by civilians on essential work to avoid them being presented with the white feather of cowardice by zealously patriotic women, so presumably he didn't serve in the armed forces. He was rumoured to have been bigamously married. I don't remember ever meeting Uncle Jim.

Reinforcing the slender cohort of real uncles was a small legion of honorary uncles. These were the men who had been my father's comrades in 'M' Company, Special Brigade of the Royal Engineers, responsible for gas warfare, and who had, like him, managed to survive the conflict. There was 'Uncle' Clem, Leonard Clements, who had been best man at G.O.M.'s wedding in September 1918. 'Uncle' Mac was Tom McIntosh, who when the war was over worked as an industrial chemist at Ferodo, the brake linings manufacturer, in Chapel-en-le-Frith, Derbyshire. 'Uncle' Jimmy was James Lambert, who became a Director of ICI Nobel Division at Ardrossan, in Scotland, and was a guest at my own first wedding to Margaret Ayres at Westminster Cathedral in July 1956. 'Uncle' Heyes was the only Catholic in the group and was invited to become my Godfather when I was born and baptised a Catholic in 1929. He was another guest at my first wedding. I suspect that he played a big part in helping my parents to decide which schools I should go to. He, too, became an industrial chemist, in Nottingham.

And there were many more. In the 1920s and 1930s, after the war was over, all the honorary uncles came together every year for 'M' Company's reunion dinner. At the menu for the dinner at the Old Hall Hotel in Chinley, Derbyshire, held on 17 September 1932, the toasts were 'The King' and 'Old Comrades'. The latter must have been especially poignant, as the survivors remembered those who never came back. I am not sure when 'M' Company's reunion dinners stopped, but 'C' Company's went on until 1981. On 25 September 1965, my father travelled from Manchester to Eastbourne for a reunion dinner for the surviving ex-soldiers of all the companies in the gas Special Brigade. On the back of the menu was a map of the Battle of Loos, which had been launched fifty years previously, to the day, and which is the subject of Chapter 6.

While my childhood home in the 1930s and 1940s was in Manchester, Lancashire, and Manchester is where I was born, it was always clear that we were a Yorkshire family, living in exile west of the Pennines. Some time in the early nineteenth century, the Mitchells had moved with their sheep from south-west Scotland to Yorkshire. By the middle of the century they were firmly established as leading players in the wool business in Bradford, at that time the world centre of the wool trade. My great-great-grandfather, John Mitchell, was the subject of a large oil portrait presented '. . . as a token of the high estimation in which he is generally held by persons frequenting the Colonial Wool Sales, 1847'. There is an accompanying subscription list, listing all the wool trade worthies who each chipped in 2s 6d (worth about £7.80 today) to pay for the picture to be painted. The painting is unsigned. There is no record of who painted it: it was an era when the subject of a picture was more important than the painter.

John Mitchell's grandson was George Arthur Mitchell, my paternal grandfather, born in 1860. At the age of 16 he was apprenticed to a fellmonger (dealer in sheepskins) in St Neots, Huntingdonshire. His letters home to his family, which have been handed down to me through the generations, reveal all the loneliness of a young lad from Yorkshire stranded in a strange, southern county. At Whitsun Bank Holiday he wishes he was back home in Bradford as he '. . . never was at such a dull place as there is no cricket'. The complaints about the dearth of cricket crop up frequently in his letters, as do comments on the poor quality of the singing in church on Sundays and the deteriorating state of his second best trousers.

When he was in his twenties, George Arthur Mitchell met a Lincolnshire girl, Emma Gathercole, at a social event in Bradford. The family tradition is that, on first seeing her across a crowded room, he exclaimed 'What a splendid woman! I shall marry her – but not until I have a carriage and pair and £1,000 a year.' The conditions seem to have been fulfilled by 1893, when they were married. G.O.M. was born the next year and his brother Rupert in 1897. Another son, Harold, was born in 1899, but died of meningitis when just a year old.

While my paternal grandfather may have been prosperous at the time of his marriage, family lore is that he was penniless at the time of his early death, aged 46, in 1906. He left behind a widow with two sons, G.O.M. aged 12, and Rupert, who was nine years old. Money was very short. With the help of a family friend, a place for Rupert was secured at the Yorkshire Society's School in London. This charitable institution had been set up as long ago as 1812 to educate boys born in Yorkshire whose parents '... must have been in a respectable line of life and now reduced by misfortune, or one or both of them dead'. It was under the patronage of the Archbishop of York and included among its presidents such Yorkshire notables as the Duke of Leeds, the Marquis of Zetland and Earl Fitzwilliam. Family legend has it that the nine-year-old Rupert, on first arriving by train at London's King's Cross station, saw his fellow passengers head towards the rank of horse-drawn hansom cabs. He promptly hailed a cab himself and instructed the cabbie to take him to the school in Westminster Bridge Road. On arrival, he had something of an altercation with the cabbie, as he had not realised that a cab ride had to be paid for, and he had no money. He was bailed out by a much displeased headmaster. Rupert stayed at the charitable school for six years, until 1913.

Back in Bradford, G.O.M. was completing his schooling at Thornton Grammar School. He entered Bradford Technical College in 1910, taking a three-year course in chemistry and dyeing and attracting an accolade from the Principal that 'He will make a competent assistant in a works laboratory.'[2] In the summer, he spent as much spare time as possible watching Yorkshire play cricket, occasionally in Bradford but more often a few miles away at the club's headquarters in Headingley, Leeds. Throughout his later life he

---

[2] After the First World War, G.O.M pursued a career as a dyestuffs chemist, finishing up as Chief Colourist of ICI Dyestuffs Division.

was a fount of tales of Wilfred Rhodes, George Herbert Hirst and other cricketing titans from an epoch when his beloved Yorkshire dominated the County Championship.[3]

G.O.M. also had an abiding love of the Edwardian music hall, delighting in Little Tich, Marie Lloyd, Albert Chevalier, Vesta Tilley, Dan Leno, George Robey and other stars whose names still resonate among the older generation today. He was word perfect in many of their songs, jokes and routines – I can still sing snatches of many of the songs myself, remembered from my childhood. G.O.M. must have spent many happy evenings at the Empire and Palace theatres in Bradford.

Somewhere in the background of G.O.M.'s life in Bradford, a large but now indeterminate presence, was J B Priestley, who later became a leading dramatist, novelist and – in a phrase that has gone out of fashion – man of letters. His name lives on primarily through his play *An Inspector Calls*, part of the school syllabus for English literature and the subject of a recent National Theatre production. I am still not sure how G.O.M. came to know Priestley. They were both born in Bradford within a few months of each other, but went to different secondary schools, G.O.M. to Thornton Grammar and Priestley to Belle Vue High School. However, they lived within a few yards of each other, G.O.M. in Jesmond Avenue and Priestley round the corner in Saltburn Place, off Toller Lane. Also, after finishing their education, both worked in the textile industry, Priestley in a firm exporting wool and G.O.M. in the application of dyestuffs to textiles, so perhaps they had a working relationship as well as being near neighbours. Priestley shared G.O.M.'s enthusiasm for both cricket and the music hall, so they may have gone together to watch Yorkshire play or to sit in the gallery at the Bradford theatres.

---

[3] G.O.M. inherited his father's love of cricket. The earliest photograph I have of him (*c.* 1905) shows him playing garden cricket with his brother Rupert (see illus. 1). In later life he had a row of *Wisden Cricketers' Almanak* on his bookshelves and was an enthusiastic supporter of Yorkshire. Until 1992, you could only play for Yorkshire if you were born in the county. When I was a teenager, my parents told me that they had planned for my mother to travel from Manchester (Lancashire) to visit her sister in Halifax when my birth was expected, so that I could be born in Yorkshire. Their plot to ensure that I was qualified to play for their beloved county was foiled by my premature arrival. It is just possible that I would never have played for Yorkshire anyway, as I was never even selected for my school First XI. However, I did to some extent redeem myself in their eyes in the summer of 1954. Seven cricket-less years after leaving school, I was roped in at the last moment one August Saturday to play for the Labour Party against the Midland Bank. It was my last and greatest innings – a match-winning 20 not out. G.O.M. was delighted that I had at long last come good, though I interpreted the outcome as the triumph of socialism over capitalism.

G.O.M. admired Priestley enormously. Priestley's novel *The Good Companions* was his favourite book, read and reread. When my father died in 1969, I wanted to keep it as a memento, but it was falling to pieces with his repeated reading. In the early days of the Second World War, G.O.M., my mother, my sister Joy and I used to gather round the wireless (radio) on Sunday evenings to listen to Priestley's *Postscript* talks, broadcast on the BBC Home Service immediately after the nine o'clock news. These were homespun, no nonsense, fireside chats, effectively counterpointing the grandiloquence of Winston Churchill's public rhetoric. They had a huge audience and a tremendous impact on morale in the dark days after the defeat at Dunkirk in May 1940. We were surprised when these immensely popular broadcasts stopped in the spring of 1941. It has subsequently been alleged that Churchill was jealous of Priestley's popularity and apprehensive of his agenda for a post-war Britain free from the unemployment and poverty of the previous two decades and that the Minister of Information, Duff Cooper, ordered the BBC to take Priestley off the air.

For G.O.M., Priestley embodied the essential British public and private virtues of the time: plain speaking, common sense, quiet humour, modesty and determination. It was a special virtue in G.O.M.'s eyes that Priestley, even though he was later a leading light in London's literary life, never lost his Bradford (pronounced 'Bratford') accent. Had my father lived long enough to read Judith Cook's biography *Priestley* (1997), he would have been delighted that his own manuscript diary of the First World War, now lodged in the Imperial War Museum (and which is the backbone of the later chapters of this book) had been one of the sources she used. Whatever the connection between the two young men from Bradford, their lives were to be changed dramatically by the events of the first week in August 1914, which saw them both go off to war. G.O.M., who had by then grown into a tall, sandy-haired young man, joined up on the day war broke out, Priestley a month or so later.

CHAPTER 2

To War

IN JUNE 1914, THE ARCHDUKE FRANZ FERDINAND, nephew of the Austrian Emperor Franz Josef and heir apparent to the throne, arrived in the recently annexed province of Bosnia to supervise the Habsburg army's summer manoeuvres. The manoeuvres themselves were something of a political provocation, since they took place up against the border with neighbouring Serbia – and Franz Ferdinand was known to be an enemy of Serbia. When the manoeuvres finished on 28 June, the Archduke and his wife, Sophie Chotek, were driven to the Bosnian provincial capital of Sarajevo, to pay a state visit.

There had been advance warnings, not least by the Serbian government, that the Archduke's presence in Bosnia would not be desirable. While Bosnia had been freed from Ottoman Turkish rule, the Slavs in the (then as now) ethnically and religiously tangled Bosnian population resented Austrian rule and sought union with Serbia. The timing of the visit seemed especially provocative to the pro-Serbian Bosnian Slavs. 28 June was not only '*Vidovdan*' (the feast day of St Vitus, their national patron saint), but also the anniversary of the first battle of Kosovo in 1389, when the Serbs had lost their empire to Ottoman Turkey. This day of sacred mourning had to some extent been redeemed as recently as October 1912, when Serbia defeated Turkey at the battle of Kumanovo, but 28 June remained a day of profound political and religious significance for Bosnian and Serbian Slavs.

An assassination squad of five young Bosnian Serbs and one Bosnian Muslim, Mehmedbashti, was waiting for the Archduke and his consort. They had trained, after a fashion, in Serbia, as part of a terrorist cell known as the 'Black Hand' and then returned across the mountainous border back into Bosnia. As Franz Ferdinand and Sophie Chotek were driven to the town hall, one of the terrorists, Cabrinovic, threw a bomb. It glanced off the royal car and then exploded, wounding an officer in the following car. Less than an hour later, the Archduke and his wife left the town hall to set off on the short but hazardous drive to the city hospital, to visit the wounded officer. Within minutes, in a moment of confusion about the route,

the car happened to stop immediately in front of another of the conspirators, Gavrilo Princip. He shot Franz Ferdinand and Sophie Chotek dead.[1]

Ever since that day, there has been speculation as to whether or not the Serbian government was directly involved in the plot. At the time, the Austrian newspapers carried extensive reports of alleged 'confessions' by the conspirators that the bomb plot had been hatched by the Serbian government. No hard evidence has ever been found to support this. Indeed, it was not in Serbia's interest to provoke a dispute with Austria-Hungary at that time. The country was in an exhausted state. In October 1912, it had allied with Bulgaria, Greece and Montenegro to inflict a whirlwind defeat on the Ottoman Empire in the First Balkan War. This had been quickly followed in the summer of 1913 by the Second Balkan War, in which Bulgaria launched a surprise attack on her previous allies in a dispute over the division of the territories that had been taken from Turkey. In 1914, Serbia was in no condition to engage in conflict, least of all against the might of Austria-Hungary.

However, the Austro-Hungarian government determined to use the assassination as a pretext for confronting what it considered to be Serbia's ambitions to become a major power – 'Greater Serbia' – in south-eastern Europe. On 23 July, it issued Serbia with a list of eleven demands that would, in effect, have turned it into an Austrian vassal state. Serbia was given just forty-eight hours to accept, though in truth it was an ultimatum that was intended to be rejected. However, so keen was Serbia to avoid war at that time that it sent a conciliatory note of agreement, accepting eight of the outrageous demands and offering to discuss the other three. This unexpectedly soft response caused some embarrassment in Vienna. However, Austria-Hungary was determined on war in any event and brushed aside Serbia's

---

[1]The marriage between Franz Ferdinand and Sophie Chotek was a love match and was contrary to the wishes of the Archduke's mother. So appalled was the Viennese Court that the heir apparent to the throne of the Austro-Hungarian Empire should choose such a low born consort, that it was ruled that their marriage should be a morganatic one – that is, that when the Archduke succeeded to the throne, Sophie Chotek would not become Empress. Moreover, Franz Ferdinand had been required to sign a humiliating undertaking renouncing the rights of any as yet unborn children of the marriage to succeed to the throne. There is no comparable provision for a morganatic marriage in English law. Nevertheless, it was canvassed as a possible solution in 1936 when Edward VII fell in love with the twice-divorced commoner, Bessie Wallis Warfield (better known as Mrs Wallis Simpson and later as the Duchess of Windsor). It was even whispered about more recently as a possibility in the case of the Prince of Wales and the once-divorced commoner, Mrs Camilla Parker-Bowles.

qualified acceptance of its demands. On 25 July, Emperor Franz Josef ordered mobilisation of the Austro-Hungarian army against Serbia and three days later declared war.

The Sarajevo assassination gave a fresh impetus to the war fever that had been intensifying in European government circles in the early years of the twentieth century. Germany used the dispute between Austria-Hungary and Serbia as the pretext for launching a European war. On 30 July, Russia mobilised its army in support of Serbia, a country with which it had historic cultural and political ties. As well as being fellow Slavs, Russians and Serbs shared a common religion, the Greek Orthodox Church, as well as the Cyrillic alphabet. Germany responded by mobilising its army on the following day and on 1 August declared war on Russia. France mobilised immediately in support of its Russian ally, but with great caution ordered that no troops should go within ten kilometres of the German border.

On 3 August Germany declared war on France and delivered an ultimatum to neutral Belgium demanding the free passage of its army to invade France. Belgium's refusal to give way led to an immediate German invasion and by 4 August the Belgian fortresses defending Liège were already under siege by the German army. That day, there was a crucial discussion in the British Cabinet. The Liberal Government had by no means been united in its policy towards Germany. A minority of Ministers, reflecting a significant element in public opinion, had been opposing the drift towards war with Germany. For a brief period, Lloyd George, at the time the influential Chancellor of the Exchequer,[2] toyed with the idea of joining them. However, the stance of the anti-war group was undermined by the German invasion of Belgium. The Cabinet decided to demand that Germany should respect Belgian neutrality and withdraw her troops. Germany's failure to respond meant that, from midnight on 4 August, Britain allied itself with France and Russia in being at war with Germany and Austria-Hungary.

The outbreak of war was the culmination of growing antagonism between Britain and Germany, a new phenomenon in the relations between two countries that had never been at war and that shared – and still share – so many national and cultural characteristics. German music, literature and philosophy were admired as some of the highest achievements of European civilization. Not least, there were close ties between the royal families of the two countries. Queen

---

[2]Later Prime Minister 1916–1922

Victoria had a German mother and married a German, Albert, the Prince Consort. One of their grandsons was Kaiser Wilhelm, the German Emperor.

However, rivalry between the two countries began to grow in the new century. It intensified after 1909 to such an extent that there was widespread speculation in political circles, not as to whether or not there would be war between the two countries, but as to when it would start. Underlying the more specific causes of the war, there was fear on both sides. Britain, France and Russia were apprehensive about Germany's hegemony in central Europe as well as its rapidly growing industrial and commercial power: Britain was specifically concerned about Germany's expanding navy. On the other side, Germany claimed she was the victim of hostile encirclement by the three great powers and that she had not got her rightful share of African territory in the great colonial land grab that took place during the last quarter of the nineteenth century.

Through the prism of history, there seems to have been a certain inevitability about the outbreak of war. The political and economic pressures all seem to have been pointing in one direction. However, it didn't seem like that to ordinary men and women at the time. In his autobiographical *Winds of Change* (1966), Harold Macmillan,[3] who was twenty years old in 1914, expresses the view that:

> The First War, in contrast to the Second, burst like a bombshell on ordinary people. It came suddenly and unexpectedly – a real 'bolt from the blue' . . . Indeed, in the summer of 1914, there was far more anxiety about a civil war in Ireland than about a world war in Europe . . . The occasional outbursts of the Kaiser were treated as pardonable indiscretions; Germany, after all, appeared to be governed by men of solid reputation and a civilised background.

However, the mould for the First World War was set. On one side, the Allies – Britain, France and Russia, supporting Belgium and Serbia, to be joined later by Japan and Italy: on the other, the 'Central Powers', Germany and Austria-Hungary, to be reinforced three months later by Turkey, the rambling Ottoman Empire which extended from the south-eastern tip of Europe on the Bosphorous all the way to the Persian Gulf. However, at the outset, few envisaged the savage character that the war would take on over the next four

---

[3]Prime Minister 1957–1963

years or the scale of death and destruction. Indeed, there was widespread ignorance about what twentieth-century war might involve. On the day that war broke out, the *Bradford Daily Argus* suggested that '... it will be in the kitchens that the pinch will be chiefly felt but that difficulty may be overcome by deleting the more dainty dishes.' Four years later, there were ten million dead.

* * *

In the afternoon of Tuesday 4 August 1914, a long green envelope dropped on to the door mat of G.O.M.'s Bradford home. It was stamped 'MOBILISATION – URGENT'. Inside was Army Form E635, requiring him to report for duty the next morning at Belle Vue barracks.

What did mobilisation mean? G.O.M. had volunteered for the Territorial Army some two or three years before the outbreak of war. The Territorial Army itself was a relatively new innovation, reconstituted in 1908 out of the ashes of the former county Volunteer and Yeomanry regiments. Popularly known as 'Saturday night soldiers', the Terriers committed themselves to a weekly training evening and an annual camp. They constituted a partially trained reserve, to be drawn on if war came, and their primary purpose was to defend Britain against a foreign invader, allowing the regular army to fight in Europe or overseas.

G.O.M. did not come from a military family and, though undemonstratively patriotic, was not in any sense a militaristic man. Why, then, had he joined the Terriers in peace time? It's difficult to know for certain at this distance in time, but the motives of many such volunteers are summarised by the Regimental historian, Laurie Magnus, in *The West Riding Territorials in the Great War* (1920), '... as a relief from the monotony of civil life, as an outlet for high spirits, and as a means of spending a healthy holiday with good comrades.' This is probably not far off the mark. A photograph of G.O.M. with his Terrier mates taken at their 1913 summer camp in Aberystwyth shows a bunch of happy, apparently carefree young men. Training it may have been, but hardly serious-minded preparation for war.

This all changed when G.O.M.'s mobilisation papers came through the letterbox. By 6 pm on Thursday 6 August the 1/6th ('first sixth') Battalion of the West Yorkshire Regiment reported that 575 men out of the battalion strength of 588 had reported for duty at Bradford's Belle Vue Barracks (see illus. 2). All received a bounty of £5 (worth some £325 in today's money), kit allowance of ten shillings (the

equivalent of £32.50 today), a pair of boots and two shirts: pay was one shilling per day (£3.25). They spent the next few nights sleeping on the floor of the Drill Hall. A medical examination weeded out no less than 20 per cent as being unfit for military duties.

Surviving photographs showing long queues of young men outside recruiting offices in the opening days of the war have created an impression that the youth of Britain flocked to join the services as soon as war broke out. This does not accord with the facts. In the month of August 1914, there were 300,000 recruits. While this inflow more than doubled the size of Britain's military strength, and was substantially greater than the 100,000 called for by Lord Kitchener, the Secretary of State for War, on 7 August, and the further 100,000 he called for towards the end of the month, it was only a small proportion of those eligible to serve – less than 5 per cent. In *The Pity of War* (1998), Niall Ferguson cites an estimate that there were at the time nearly six and a half million men of military age.

On 8 August, G.O.M.'s battalion sent in an official report to headquarters that it was up to its full wartime establishment, with 29 officers, 979 men and all necessary transport. Fifty-seven horses had been bought. Ten were for the officers to ride, the rest to pull the wagons that constituted the battalion's transport in those days. Motorised lorries did not come on the scene until later in the war. It was a matter of great regimental pride that it was the first Territorial unit in the country to be fully mobilised and ready to move.

At 7.30 am on Tuesday 11 August, G.O.M. and his younger brother Rupert, who had enlisted under age at 16 years and ten months, marched with the rest of the battalion from Belle Vue Barracks to Bradford's Midland Station (see illus. 3). The column must have looked a fine sight, each company headed by mounted officers in their jodhpurs, polished riding boots and shining spurs, swords swinging at their sides. The men in their stiff flat caps, gleaming brass badges and buttons, with khaki puttees wound round their ankles, marched in columns four abreast, rifles at the slope on their shoulders. They were followed by a procession of horse-drawn wagons laden with ammunition, tents and supplies. They were ideally equipped for war – for the South African Boer War, that is, which had ended twelve years previously.

There were rumours that the battalion was bound for Tilbury Docks, with Egypt or India as their eventual destination. Contrary to

the stereotype imprinted on later generations by photographs and old newsreel pictures of the British army going off to war in 1914, the battalion left its home city almost unobserved – 'The bands did not play, there were no cheering crowds, no interested spectators.' Battalion Orders had made it clear that families and friends would not be allowed into the station. The rumours of the exotic Orient proved unfounded when, after a journey of thirty miles or so, the train came to a halt at Selby – east of Bradford, certainly, but still in Yorkshire.

Six months of training in camp at various places in Yorkshire, including Strensall and the Knavesmire Racecourse at York, were interspersed with coastal defence duties in the Redcar area. It was here that G.O.M. and his comrades, though not themselves under fire, first heard the rumbling of guns fired in anger. On 16 December 1914, a little more than four months after the outbreak of war, ships of the German High Seas Fleet bombarded the nearby east coast towns of Hartlepool, Whitby and Scarborough. Hartlepool was a shipbuilding town with some rudimentary coastal defences – three elderly and inadequate six-inch guns, manned by a territorial unit. Whitby, then as now, was a quaint small fishing port and an attractive spot for tourists and holidaymakers. Scarborough was a rather grand seaside resort, popular as a retirement haven for exhausted Yorkshire pensioners. Whitby and Scarborough had no military installations or industrial factories and were completely undefended.

The attacks caused considerable damage and many casualties. According to Richard van Emden and Steve Humphries in *All Quiet on the Home Front* (2003), 1,500 shells rained down on Hartlepool in fifty minutes. As well as nine soldiers, 97 men and women were killed and 37 children. There were 466 wounded. In Whitby and Scarborough, there were 21 dead and 100 wounded. They were the first British civilian casualties of the war. There was universal outrage at this example of 'Hunnish atrocity'. At a deeper level, there was a sense of loss of innocence. While the British army had come to terms with the desperate reality of twentieth-century warfare during the retreat from Mons and the Battles of the Aisne and the Marne in the autumn of 1914, the war had not yet really impinged on civilian life. The shelling of the three coastal towns was a brutal awakening. The supposedly invincible British navy was nowhere to be seen and had proved incapable of defending Britain's shores. For the civilian population of Britain, it was this assault rather than the outbreak of war four months earlier that marked the end of a golden age,

epitomised in the title of Osbert Sitwell's novel about the shelling of
Scarborough, *Before the Bombardment* (1926).[4]

Back at the inland Yorkshire base of G.O.M.'s battalion, there
had been a further weeding out of thirty-eight men as physically
unfit, with ten more recruits being sent home labelled as 'undesir-
able'. The official record notes that enlistment was done at such
high speed in mobilisation '. . . that it was impossible to inquire into
the characters of many of the men'. Following a move to
Gainsborough in Lincolnshire on 26 February 1915, forty-five more
men were declared unfit. The high proportion of men who were
rejected on physical grounds was pervasive throughout the country –
and these were volunteers, who had already been subject to
part-time training. When conscription was introduced in 1916, a
national check showed that, of every nine men examined, only three
were A1 fit. Of the remainder, two were of inferior health, three
incapable and one a permanent invalid. Overall, 41 per cent of
young men were given the lowest health classification of C3. These
figures throw into sharp relief the abysmal living conditions and
widespread malnutrition of the industrial working class in a country
supposedly passing through an era of prosperity, and one which was
still the wealthiest in the world. The average height of recruits who
were accepted was barely five feet six inches. G.O.M., who
measured six feet, was very tall for his generation and must have
stood out from the crowd.

Another filter was provided by the Territorial terms of service.
Anyone joining a Territorial unit signed on for a fixed period of five
years of home service within Britain. He could only be sent to Europe
or overseas if he agreed to what was known as the Imperial Service
Obligation. This was a quite different arrangement from the 'New
Army' units being formed in response to Kitchener's call to arms. The
New Army volunteers undertook to serve for as long as the war lasted
and in any theatre of war. As it prepared to go to France, the 1/6th
Battalion comprised only those who had undertaken the Imperial

---

[4]Osbert Sitwell's family home at the time was Wood End, Scarborough. When the attack took
place, he himself was serving with the Grenadier Guards at Chelsea Barracks in London,
preparing for embarkation to France. In his biography of Edith, Osbert and Sacheverell Sitwell,
Façades (1978), John Pearson writes that, as fragments of German shells struck the family
home, their father, Sir George Sitwell sheltered in the cellar while their mother, Lady Ida,
remained resolutely in bed, defying the German fleet: 'According to Osbert, Sir George would
always be convinced that he had been one of the prime targets of the Germans, and that he
had endured a worse bombardment than any that his son was to face at the front.'

1. G.O.M. (left) and his younger brother Rupert c. 1905

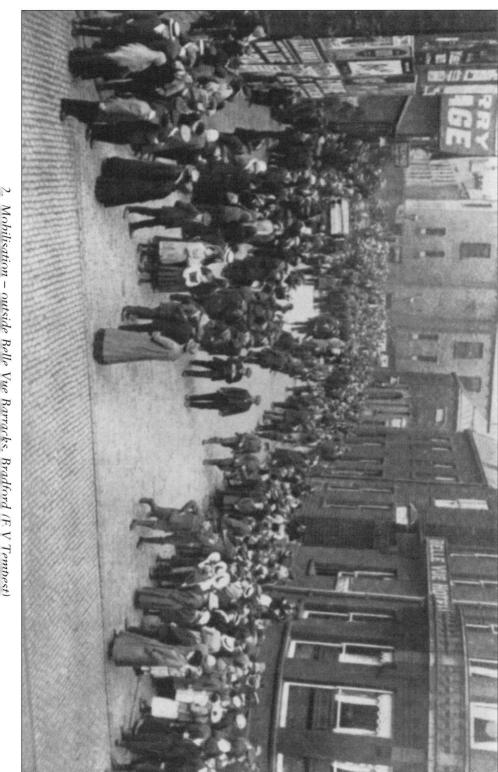

2. Mobilisation – outside Belle Vue Barracks, Bradford (E V Tempest)

3. 1/6th Battalion West Yorkshire Regiment preparing to leave Bradford (E V Tempest)

4. In the front line for the first time – Fauquissart. Sandbag ramparts were used for protection as the high water table made it impossible to dig trenches. (E. V. Tanbart)

5. *Ruins of the Cloth Hall and Cathedral, Ypres (IWM Q2920)*

6. *German troops in gas masks (IWM Q53091)*

7. *Troops advancing through a gas and smoke cloud (IWM Q69586)*

8. RE Special Company members at revolver practice, Helfaut base (REM)

9. Gas cylinders in a front line trench ready to be discharged (IWM Q57917)

Service Obligation. Those who had not – mostly married men with children – were allocated to home service units.

Training and preparation came to an end on 15 April, when the 1/6th Battalion of the West Yorkshires left Gainsborough for Folkestone in two special trains. They travelled via Lincoln and London Liverpool Street. In marked contrast to their low-key departure from their home city of Bradford eight months earlier, they were greeted by cheering crowds on the platforms of the stations they passed through. However, morale received something of a jolt on the way. While the train stopped at Liverpool Street the evening papers being sold on the platform printed lengthy casualty lists of the recent battle of Neuve Chapelle, in which 11,000 British soldiers were killed, wounded, missing or prisoners of war.[5]

The trains arrived at Folkestone at 8 pm and the battalion embarked straight away on the SS *Victoria*. With all lights extinguished and an escort of torpedo boats, the troopship set sail for France. After a calm crossing, they reached Boulogne at 11 pm. G.O.M. records in his diary that 'As the boat drew near to the quay, every one of us gazed intently upon this, for many, new land': he himself had spent a pre-war family holiday at nearby Wimereux and was one of the few to have a smattering of French. Carrying rifles and full kit, the men then had a stiff two and a half miles march up the hill behind the port to the St Martin's rest camp, finally bedding down in their greatcoats – on grass but under canvas – at 2 am the next morning. For many, it was not just the first night they had spent outside England, but their first night away from Yorkshire.

Next morning, G.O.M. and his comrades paraded early and marched four miles under the blazing sun to the station at Pont de Briques, outside Boulogne. Unlike the comfortable passenger train that had taken them from Gainsborough to Folkestone, the train waiting to take them to Merville consisted of goods wagons. Each wagon was labelled 'Hommes 40 Chevaux 8' (40 Men 8 Horses), so forty men with their rifles and full packs were allocated to each truck. There was no room to stand or sit properly. What G.O.M. described as the 'horrible journey' via Calais and Hazebrouck, where a hospital

---

[5] These lists foretold the shape of things to come for the West Yorkshires. By the end of the Battle of the Somme in 1916, only a handful of the original 1/6th Bn Territorial officers and men who embarked at Folkestone in April 1915 had survived unscathed. When eventually the Armistice was signed on 11 November 1918, the Battalion had over three and a half years in the trenches suffered more than 139 battle casualties among its officers and 2,038 among its other ranks – more than four times its average strength.

train full of wounded coming back from the front was a sobering sight, took eight hours to crawl the eighty miles.

Merville was some twelve miles from the front line, west of Lille, which was in German hands. They arrived in pitch darkness and driving rain. G.O.M. '. . . could see flares (a long way off) and hear an occasional gun'. Wet and cold, they marched towards the hamlet of Le Sart. Chaos ensued as the column was enveloped in darkness and the horse-drawn transport wagons and limbers (two-wheeled ammunition carriages) sank to their axles in the mud. G.O.M. 'had a hell of a job manhandling some limbers as far as the transport lines . . . no lights of course, semi-wild mules and a frisky horse were some of the drawbacks'.

The battalion was supposed to be billeted on the frightened villagers of Le Sart, trying to carry on their normal lives within earshot of the front line gunfire, but in the darkness no one could find their proper billet in the scattered settlement. One company commander fell into an open sewer up to his armpits and was only dragged out with difficulty, providing the rain-sodden soldiers with welcome light relief. G.O.M. eventually slept in a stable, alongside the resident livestock. There were forty or fifty men to each farmyard.

During the several days they spent in Le Sart, G.O.M. and his comrades continued to live in barns and stables, sleeping in hay and straw, with a single blanket each. It was so cold that there was continual movement throughout the night, as men got up to walk around and bring warmth to their frozen limbs. In spite of the cold, no fires were allowed, because of the fire risk from hay and straw. Indeed, the barn and stable buildings were themselves inflammable, as they were built, not from brick or stone, but from wooden laths covered with baked clay – a building technique also found in the East Anglian fens. In one barn, the floor of the rickety loft gave way and half a dozen men fell on to the horses fifteen feet below. In spite of the primitive conditions, the men were expected to parade with polished boots and shining brass buttons. G.O.M. comments that his friend F W Whitaker was 'crimed' (put on a disciplinary charge) for dirty boots. G.O.M. managed to see his brother Rupert, who was in a different company, nearly every day.

The battalion marched eastwards out of Le Sart on Thursday 22 April, through La Gorgue to the small industrial town of Estaires, some six miles nearer the front line, which had been occupied by the Germans for eight days in October 1914 before being recaptured. The following Wednesday, G.O.M. reports:

Plenty of subdued excitement. Rumour that we were going in [to the front line] proved to be true. Marched off at 6 pm. Went through Laventie, which had been thoroughly shelled. Practically everything in ruins. Terrible desolation.

Before the war, Laventie had been a pleasant little town, with wide, tree-lined streets, villas, a *mairie* (town hall) and other public buildings.

They marched on past Dead Man's Corner to the ruined village of Fauquissart. At last, they had reached the front line.

Chapter 3

The Front Line

Fauquissart was to be g.o.m.'s first experience of front line combat. In many ways, the area was not typical of conditions on the Western Front. The nature of the terrain made trench warfare impossible, because of flooding. The countryside was flat, with a high water table. The fields were bordered by dykes, rather than hedges, lined with poplars and willows. The British and German front line positions were about 150 to 200 yards apart. In between was the Rivière des Laies, which was not in fact a river but a man-made drainage dyke. This was normally about fifteen feet wide, but when the rain came down it flooded both front lines. To G.O.M.'s surprise. 'Trenches not what I thought they were. Not a trench at all, but merely a sand-bag parapet, about 6–7 feet high and 3–5 feet thick. Except for low parados [behind the firing position] everything open at the back.' The men lived in lean-to shelters behind the front parapet (see illus. 4). There were no communication trenches. Men and supplies had to be moved at night across virtually open country.

Fauquissart was also not typical in that the countryside was relatively unscarred and was still being worked by the local farmers not far behind the front lines. There was fruit in the orchards. Wild flowers grew in the fields. Nightingales could be heard in the morning. However, appearances were deceptive. During the day, there was occasional sniping, punctuated by bursts of machine-gun fire – 'Bullets occasionally whistled [by].' G.O.M. felt the adrenalin of battle: 'Curious feeling of elation as was my first time under fire.'

This first taste of life in the front line, which lasted twenty-four hours, proved to be relatively uneventful. 'Very little enemy rifle fire, but a deuce of a lot by us. Quite understandable.' One moment of excitement was when one of our planes dropped a bomb on the German lines. This was quite a rare occurrence at the time, as at this stage of the war the wood-and-wire biplanes were used by both sides mainly for aerial photography and artillery observation.

In his *History of the 6th Battalion West Yorkshire Regiment Volume I 1/6th Battalion* (1921), the Battalion historian, Captain

E V Tempest, fills out the detail of this first encounter with the reality of trench warfare:

> Everyone was impressed with the morning and evening 'Stand-to'. At the approach of dusk the word was rapidly passed down to all ranks by the officer and NCO [Non-Commissioned Officer] on duty and the trench became the scene of sudden activity. Men came out of dugouts, and got up from the firesteps where they had been resting: examined rifles and bayonets: looked at their ammunition: prepared for the unknown adventures of the night. Sentries loosed off a few rounds at the enemy: MGs [machine guns] fired one or two rounds from their night emplacements (the MGs were strictly rationed in ammunition in those days!). The enemy replied and a desultory fire began along the whole front . . . Then the first star shells were sent up: after which minutes passed uneventfully: darkness came on rapidly, and the sentries could not see beyond their own wire: there was 'nothing doing'. Men said to each other, 'Fritz seems quiet enough to-night.' The hour of danger passed, and the order was given to 'stand down'. The trenches again became silent, except for the whispered talk of sentries: the occasional rat-tat-tat of an MG: or a sentry's rifle-fire, caused by a suspected enemy patrol, or a desire to keep himself awake during the two or three hours' watch.
>
> The first night in the line seemed long to our men: the dawn inexpressibly grateful. Again the 'stand-to' order was passed down the line: all patrols were in: the enemy's trenches could be dimly seen through the mist. Rifles and ammunition were again examined: everyone was again on the alert during the dangerous hour when there is enough light to guide men for a big attack, yet enough darkness to give shelter from accurate fire. There followed the usual 'morning hate'. Those hours from dawn to breakfast were nearly always the worst part of the day for the wretched infantryman . . . they shelled us merrily and registered fairly good hits.

The West Yorkshires were relieved in the evening of the following day, Thursday 29 April, after their first short taste of life in the front line. There had been seven casualties, all wounded. For the first time, G.O.M. had heard the cry 'Stretcher bearers!' though the fighting had not been intense by later standards. G.O.M. noted that he and his comrades '. . . had a very exhausting march back [to their reserve billets at Estaires]. Just about had enough when we landed back at the old billet, due to excitement and no sleep for about 40 hours.'

The next day they spent cleaning up and parading for inspection. A significant detail, the men were ordered to take the wires out of their service caps: the stiffened, circular flat service cap showed up

very clearly in silhouette and presented an easy target for enemy snipers. Steel helmets were still unknown at this early stage of the war, so heads were completely unprotected against enemy bullets or shrapnel. In quieter moments, G.O.M. compared notes on their first experience in battle with his brother Rupert and friend Whitaker. However, this spell behind the front line was not without excitement. 'Hun plane dropped a bomb. Missed B Company's billet by a yard and failed to explode.'

On Sunday 2 May the battalion marched the four miles from Estaires to Bac St Maur, where G.O.M. was billeted in a school. His diary for Monday 3 May 1915 carries the single, poignant entry 'My 21st birthday.'

Two days later, on Wednesday, they set off in the rain for the trenches in the Neuve Chapelle sector of the line. G.O.M.'s diary records the kind of unglamorous incident that characterised the weary years of war. Ordered to report for ration duty, he went with a comrade to the Quartermaster's stores to wait for the rations, which didn't arrive until 11 pm:

> Struggled with rations on a truck on light railway. Not enough men. Set off up communications trench, self and another struggling with crate of dixies [rectangular mess tins for cooking and eating]. An absolute maze of trenches, mostly German [British troops had recaptured the first four lines of German trenches]. Hopelessly lost but kept on until absolutely fagged out. Full pack and rifle. Abandoned dixies after 2 miles and finally staggered in our section of trench at 5 am on Thurs.

On top of the weight of the rifle, a full pack weighed at least 56 pounds, half a hundredweight. No wonder G.O.M. and his comrade struggled with the company's rations.

While there were many similarities with Fauquissart a couple of miles to the north – breastworks rather than trenches, for example – there was one major difference. The ground had been heavily fought over in the Battle of Neuve Chapelle, which had taken place just under eight weeks earlier, from 10 to 13 March 1915. In one of the most ferocious battles of the war to date, British and Indian troops had advanced across a front 8,000 yards wide and recaptured the ruined village of Neuve Chapelle. They succeeded in advancing the front line about 1,000 yards. The battle had been considered a success by the Commander of the First Army, Sir Douglas Haig. However, the Commmander-in-Chief, Sir John French, attributed the failure to

achieve the capture of Aubers Ridge, a mile or so to the east, to the shortage of shells and other ammunition and berated the War Office, leading to a public row in Parliament and the press.

In the three days that the battle lasted, there had been huge casualties on both sides. It was some of the wounded from Neuve Chapelle that G.O.M. had seen when passing the hospital train in Hazebrouck station, the day after he landed in France. The number of British and Indian troops killed, wounded, missing and taken prisoner numbered 11,652. The German total was about 8,600. The bodies of the unburied dead still lay everywhere, nearly two months later. When morning came on Thursday 6 May, G.O.M. '... found trenches (again breastworks) and ground all around absolutely foul; the smell was sickening ... Still a lot of bodies lying around after battle.'

The historian of the 1/6th Battalion, Captain E V Tempest, spells out this horrific scene in detail.

> In front of the line lay the dead, rows and rows of them, mostly British, though German dead lay thickly enough in some parts. What is the most enduring memory of the Neuve Chapelle sector? There could be only one reply: 'The Dead'. Our men existed for ten days in a vast cemetery where no one had been buried. In front and behind the line, along communication trenches, everywhere, putrescent bodies! The parapets were built up with them: they served as directing points to dugouts and sentry posts, and even helped to give direction to patrols across No Man's Land. The heavy, sickly stench, which could be felt miles away, lay in a cloud over the trenches where men ate and slept ... A peculiar callousness to the dead came over everybody. Their bodies were rifled for useful parts of equipment, matches and cigarettes ... The only difficulty was that the dead lay out in No Man's Land ...

For the first time, in Captain Tempest's words, the West Yorkshires confronted the terrible human cost of large scale trench warfare:

> Men became initiated to the strange effects of shell fire and other methods of killing men. Some men had been torn by bullets, bombs and shells till their bodies were unrecognisable; others had been untouched, dead from concussion. Some had been killed in the midst of fight, every muscle stretched; some seemed literally to have fallen asleep, with a smile. Wherever possible, they were buried, and though it was done in haste, there was no lack of sympathy ... Our men knew it was quite possible they, too, would quickly share the same fate ...

On Friday 7 May, G.O.M.'s platoon moved up to take over an advanced outpost known from its shape as 'The Duck's Bill'. The

normal trench system consisted of a front line trench with a similar support or reserve trench some distance to the rear. At right angles between the two ran communications trenches that allowed troops and supplies to be moved in both directions. All trenches were dug in irregular zigzags. However, the Duck's Bill projected out from the front of the British first line trench into No Man's Land. To G.O.M. it was 'Hell Fire Circus', an exposed position surrounded on three sides by German trenches as little as ninety yards away. It was the most dangerous spot in the Neuve Chapelle sector – 'The hottest place I was ever in or want to be in – fire from three sides. Latrines under fire.'

Tension was aggravated by the general belief that in the Duck's Bill they were crouching on top of a network of enemy tunnels and that the whole place might be blown up by mines at any moment. Also, G.O.M. and his comrades experienced for the first time bombardment by trench mortars. These were short range, high angle weapons firing small shells from the German front line trenches. They could be heard to go 'plop' when fired, sending the West Yorkshires scurrying for any cover they could find before the shells exploded.

On Sunday 9 May, the 1/6th Battalion found itself playing a minor part in a major offensive by British and French troops. This had been planned by Sir John French and the French General Foch, at that time Commander of the French Northern Group of Armies and subsequently Allied Commander-in-Chief. Their objective was to break through on a wide front south of Lille. The role of the British 49th Division, of which the 1/6th Battalion West Yorkshire Regiment was a part, was to follow up and occupy new ground if the initial attack was successful.

In the Duck's Bill outpost, G.O.M. heard a 'Terrific bombardment [which] opened at 5 am till 6 am. Violent artillery fire also infantry fire.' British troops were attacking at Fromelles on the left flank and Festubert on the immediate right. 'We were ready to go over in case attack succeeded.' However, it did not. One of the reasons was that the arrangements for the attack were not kept secret and were widely known not only among the troops but also by the French civilian population. The Germans were fully aware of and prepared for the impending attack. Indeed, on the previous day, in full view of the British front line, they had posted huge notices in front of their trenches with the words 'YOUR ATTACK POSTPONED UNTIL TOMORROW.'

The Germans were ready and waiting and the attack was a total failure. In the words of the Regimental historian, Laurie Magnus :

The first day's programme was thrown out from the start . . . The advance was broken into little pockets and blood-spots of fighting . . . The record of every fighting unit tells the same tale of desperate valour; of a few exhausted and staggering survivors hardly able to remember their own exploits, of endurance strained to the limit of capacity, and of unwilling admiration extorted even from a grudging foe.

In spite of the noise of the bombardment there had been too few guns and too few shells to destroy the enemy's barbed wire and break down the defences. The German machine guns dominated the battlefield. They opened up as soon as the British troops came out from behind their parapets. Most of those who were killed and injured were shot down in No Man's Land before they even reached the first German trench. By seven in the morning the attack had come to a standstill. The terrible news quickly came back to G.O.M. and his comrades – '. . . heard that attack had been a failure. 8th Division suffered heavily. Very depressed at news.' The total British casualties from one day's fighting on a narrow front had been 458 officers and over 11,000 men, a staggering total.

That afternoon, G.O.M.'s platoon came out of the exposed Duck's Bill but they were not far from the action and still manning the front line. Two days later, his friend Whitaker was badly wounded and '. . . got his right eye knocked out by a ricochet off parapet. Very calm about it.'[1] On Thursday 13 May, G.O.M. was briefly back in the Duck's Bill, on a Royal Engineers fatigue duty bringing up supplies of timber and corrugated iron to prop up the defensive parapets. It was still a hot spot: 'Laid in mud on road to avoid machine-gun fire. Deuce of a time.' This dangerous supply run had to be repeated the following day but, thankfully, it was 'Not quite as bad this time.'

On Saturday 15 May, after eight days under fire in the front line, the Battalion was relieved and marched back to Laventie, where G.O.M. again slept in a barn for two nights. The respite was very short, for by the middle of the following week they were back in the front line at La Cordonnerie farm, near the ruined village of

---

[1]Undeterred by his wound, G.O.M.'s friend F W Whitaker was commissioned less than two months later. He rose to be Captain, commanding 'C' Company, and was awarded the Military Cross. He later played a notable part in the major battle near Ypres on 25 April 1918, part of the last convulsive effort by the Germans to break through Allied lines. He was lucky to be captured and made prisoner of war by the Germans, because the 1/6th Battalion of the West Yorks was virtually wiped out as a fighting unit in successfully resisting the attack. Their casualties were 22 officers and 457 other ranks. After the battle, they were left with 17 officers and 110 other ranks – many of these survivors were in fact headquarters troops who had not been involved in the fighting.

Fromelles.[2] 'Trenches in a fearful condition. Raining. No dugouts. Order issued – no men allowed in dugouts at night. When not on sentry, must do necessary work at night.' G.O.M.'s wry comment is 'Rather humorous'.

However, on looking round he '... found a terrible scene of desolation. This was the scene of battle on 9 May ... A few bodies around and lots of graves. An awful smell of death and disaster. German trench mortars very active.' Over the next few days, G.O.M reports that two of his friends were wounded and that he 'Spent an awful night in a listening post (barricaded sap-head). Battalion fired 20 rounds rapid over our heads. Huns replied. Terrific racket. Trench mortars coming at us. Talk about nerves!'

The night of Monday 24 May was marked in G.O.M.'s words by '... a thunder storm, artillery duel, rapid machine-gun fire from Huns. Simply prayed for day-break. Talk about having the wind up!' In fact, night-time was rarely an opportunity to get some sleep or to rest. Frequently, the sky was lit with bursts of star shells or flares. Real or imagined figures would appear in No Man's Land, precipitating from either side – or both – a fusillade of machine-gun and rifle fire. The artillery would be called up to lay down a barrage. They might be sent out on patrol to see what was happening, which usually meant crawling from one shell hole to the next in No Man's Land. Even when things were quiet, and there was no enemy movement to attract the sentries' attention, there was endless work to be done – repairing trenches, filling and positioning sandbags, bringing up supplies, sending back the wounded.

G.O.M. and his comrades were relieved the following day '... having been 18 days out of 20 actually in the trenches'. In view of the ferocity of the fighting, the contrast between conditions in the trenches and life in Armentières – little more than two miles away – must have been surreal. When out of the front line, soldiers were sometimes able to get a permit to visit the town or to go there to collect rations. Captain E V Tempest, describes it as being at this time:

> ... one of the liveliest towns in France ... life was carried on under normal conditions. Anything could be bought there. Burberrys, with

---

[2]One of the German regiments in the front line opposite G.O.M. at Fromelles was the Bavarian Reserve Infantry Regiment, known as the 'List' Regiment, from the name of its first commander. One of the List Regiment's dispatch runners was Corporal Adolf Hitler, who was wounded by a British shell and awarded the Iron Cross, First Class.

their usual initiative, had established a branch in the town. Tennis by day, dancing by night: restaurants and cafés always crowded . . . One of our officers described the town as being 'as gay as Paris'.

G.O.M. doesn't seem to have been one of the lucky ones. Games of tennis do not feature in his diary of life in the trenches. However, Armentières entered into our family's collective memory through the famous marching song *Mademoiselle from Armentières, Parlay-vous?* My elder sister, Joy, once told me how she remembered me as an infant being bounced on G.O.M.'s knee as he sang one of the politer variants.

Coming out of the trenches, G.O.M. and his comrades spent three days resting in their reserve billets just behind the lines. 'Rest' is a comparative word in this context – one night he was called out at 1 am in the morning to dig trenches, finishing at 8 am. Then they were moved up to the front line again, this time at Bois Grenier, in the Fleurbaix sector a couple of miles south of Armentières, from Saturday 29 May to Friday 4 June 1915. The trenches were 'Quite decent' and it was a relatively uneventful time, apart from an expedition one night into No Man's Land between the British and German front line trenches to repair barbed wire, which made G.O.M. 'Very excited'.

Paradoxically, life proved to be more dangerous for G.O.M. one night when they had moved into their reserve billets at Croix Blanche. 'Our platoon in loft. All in bed, when German gun opened on a battery behind us. Three shells in our vicinity. Last one clean through roof of our loft. Talk about quitting!' Fortunately, the direct hit had been a dud, failing to explode. There was a further remove to reserve dugouts near the Battalion HQ on Thursday 10 June '. . . simply for the purpose of fatigue [duties]. Stood to each morning and then either on carrying fatigues or improving communication trench.' G.O.M. thought this was a 'Very easy time on the whole' even though 'Shelling (slight) took place occasionally.'

There was a further move in the interminable shuffling about between positions on Wednesday 16 June, when they went into billets near the Estaminet aux Cyclistes (Cyclists' Café) at Croix Blanche, in the Fleurbaix sector. He was able to meet his brother Rupert, who was in 'A' Company. Behind the front line, they had been shelled by a German artillery battery whose object was an anti-aircraft gun nearby. 'Hot 1/4 hour. Few men wounded. Gun hit.'

Six days later, G.O.M. was back in the front line, about 150 yards from the German trenches. However, a disused mine head which was

their forward position was much closer, only seventy yards away. G.O.M.:

> Went out wiring on the Wednesday (23rd) night with BD [Billy Dennis] and ER [Ernest Ruffe] at the 70 yds spot. After working for a time, Billy spotted Huns – evidently on patrol creeping back to their trenches. We quietly but firmly left and got back in trench. Few minutes later, firework display and rapid fire by Huns at 70 yds spot! More luck.

On Friday 25 June, after a very heavy thunderstorm, G.O.M. received an order to go to Fort 23 to see a gas demonstration. It was not easy to get back – 'Communication trench in an awful state. Over the ankles in mud and water. Found Fort 23 and a deuce of a lot of officers. Lecture from one officer on gas helmets etc. Got back to trenches just in time to find tea finished.' Trench life involved lengthy periods of monotony, boredom and discomfort, punctuated by vivid bursts of action. Breakfast, dinner (at midday) and tea (the evening meal), however sketchy, assume enormous importance for front line infantry confined to their trenches, just as they do for hospital patients restricted to their beds.

Late that night, they were relieved and set off on a five miles' march back to Sailly-sur-la-Lys, where the whole Battalion was billeted in one large farm. On the way, G.O.M. 'Had to halt halfway down trench, so tired' and found the farm buildings 'Very crowded'. This wasn't surprising, as there were nearly 1,000 men trying to get some sleep there.

The following evening, they marched back another four miles west to Le Doulieu, which G.O.M. found to be:

> A nice little place, chiefly remarkable for the fact that the church (which must have been a beautiful edifice) had been burnt down by the Germans (using petrol) in the early part of the war. Several places, e.g. Sailly, Croix du Bac, and Doulieu, where I have been, have been remarkable for the fact that the village itself had been left untouched, but the church had been destroyed. Good example of Hunnish frightfulness.

His platoon was billeted over a café – 'Rather crowded but best billet we'd had in France.'

Captain Tempest writes that the Mayor of Le Doulieu was very friendly and keen to show interest and hospitality. As the battalion was marching out of the town the next day, he asked the band to play the national anthem. The band struck up *God Save the King* and all

marched smartly at attention. The mayor was puzzled and disap-
pointed – 'But I wanted *Tipperary*, your proper National Anthem.'
The band responded with *It's a Long Way to Tipperary*, to the
Mayor's great pleasure.

Since its arrival in the front line ten weeks earlier, the 1/6th
Battalion West Yorkshire Regiment, forming part of the 49th (West
Riding) Division, had occupied various positions in what was known
as the Fleurbaix sector, south west of Lille. Now, the Battalion had
been pulled right out of this sector and was under orders to march
north. It was destined to fight in the Ypres salient although at this
stage it was 'destination unknown.' G.O.M. and his comrades from
Bradford were about to embark on a new phase of their war.

CHAPTER 4

'Barking against Thunder'

THE GERMAN INVASION OF BELGIUM in August 1914 was based on the principles set out in the 'Schlieffen Plan'. General Alfred von Schlieffen was appointed Chief of the German Great General Staff in 1891 and devoted himself to preparing his 'Great Memorandum' of 1905, which set out the strategy he believed would lead Germany to victory, first over France, then over Russia. Even after Schlieffen's retirement in 1905, his Plan dominated the thinking of the German General Staff. It involved a huge pincer movement. In the north, the German army would make a massive thrust through Belgium to the French channel ports of Dunkirk, Calais and Boulogne, then swing south in a great arc to capture Paris from the west and outflank the French army from behind. Meanwhile, further south in the Vosges mountains, other German formations would press heavily against the French front line. These were the two arms of the pincer. What remained of the French army would be trapped between Paris and the frontier and defeated in battle.

The Plan was meticulously timetabled. The advancing German troops in the north would slice through Belgium and reach the French frontier by the end of the third week after mobilisation. By the end of the first month, they would be deep in north-eastern France, along the line of the Somme and Meuse rivers, south of Boulogne. By the end of six weeks, the war in the west would be won. The victorious German army would then be moved by rail to the east, to attack Russia.

Initially, everything seemed to go right for General Helmuth von Moltke (the Younger), Schlieffen's successor as Chief of the German General Staff. In the north the rapid advance through Belgium continued, in spite of unexpectedly fierce resistance from the ill-equipped Belgian army, until by the first week in September advance German troops were less than fifty miles from Calais. However, at this stage the main fighting was taking place further south. German forces, after being temporarily halted by British and French troops at the Battle of Mons, had reached the Marne Valley, just thirty miles from Paris.

On 8 September, the sixty-five year old General Ferdinand Foch drafted his legendary signal to the French and British troops defending Paris – '*Mon centre cède, ma droite recule, situation excellente, j'attaque*' (My centre is giving way, my right is retreating, situation excellent, I am attacking). The tide turned. The German army was pushed back far enough to ensure that Paris was not in immediate danger. The spotlight of war switched back to the north, and in particular to Ypres.

In the summer of 1914, before war broke out, Ypres (today known by its Flemish name, Ieper) was an unassuming small town in north-west Belgium. It had not always been so. In the thirteenth and fourteenth centuries, Ypres had been a major centre of the cloth trade, rivalling the neighbouring cities of Ghent (Gand) and Bruges (Brugge) – the Flanders equivalent of Norwich or Bury St Edmunds. It still had two highly visible survivors from its days of glory, the Cloth Hall (Lakenhalle) and St Martin's Cathedral, both masterpieces of medi-aeval Gothic architecture.

By early September 1914, Ypres suddenly assumed immense strategic importance. For the Allies, it was the last chance to stem the German advance and prevent it driving through to the Channel ports of Dunkirk, Calais and Boulogne, vital links in the supply chain between Britain and France. A string of defences was hastily constructed in a thirty-five mile semi-circle east of the town, manned mainly by the British Expeditionary Force (BEF), predominantly the regular army with which Britain entered the war. German troops occupied a string of low ridges five miles or so to the east – Passchendaele, Broodseinde, Gheluvelt, Messines, all names that were to become only too familiar battlegrounds throughout the war, as both sides fought to dominate the higher ground. This sector of the front focused on Ypres was known as the Ypres Salient.

On 14 October 1914, the German army launched a massive offensive against the Ypres Salient. Within days, the Cloth Hall and the Cathedral, along with the rest of the town, had been reduced to rubble by German artillery (see illus. 5). 'First Ypres', as this battle came to be known, lasted until 22 November. The town remained in allied hands but the casualties were enormous. Writing shortly afterwards in his book *Khaki Vignettes* (1917), P J Fisher, who had served as a Church of England chaplain with the British army, labelled Ypres 'The City of the Dead'.

Twenty-four thousand British soldiers were killed in an action that in effect saw the obliteration of the BEF – British Expeditionary

Force, those elements of the regular army that had been sent to northern France following the outbreak of war. This was more than four times the total number of British soldiers killed in action in the Boer War in South Africa at the turn of the century. Going into battle, the BEF was 160,000 strong. Within just over five weeks, half had been killed, wounded or taken prisoner.

The carnage was even worse on the German side: 40–50,000 German soldiers died in the battle. This was greater than the total of German losses in the whole of the 1870 Franco-Prussian War. However, by contrast with the British regular soldiers, many of the German dead were *gymnasia* (high school) and university students who had volunteered enthusiastically only two or three months previously – indeed, *gymnasia* students were given permission to take their exams early so that they could join up. In his masterly account of the events of 1914-18, *The First World War* (1998), John Keegan writes that the nearby German cemetery at Langemark contains the graves of 25,000 German student soldiers and that its gateway is decorated with the arms of every university in Germany. The battle became known as '*Kindermord bei Ypern*' (Massacre of the Innocents at Ypres) and gave an immense psychological shock to the German people, who had been conditioned to expect a quick and virtually painless victory.

As winter drew in, the 'Western Front' solidified into lines of trenches weaving south for more than 450 miles from Nieuport, on the Belgian coast, to the Swiss frontier. With offensives by either side gaining and losing a few miles here and there, it was to remain that way for four bloody and weary years. The Ypres Salient continued to be a focal point of fighting in the north. It was again fiercely attacked by German troops in the spring of 1915, when they fought their way to within two miles of the ruined centre of the town – 'Second Ypres'. Then and later, the defences held, right through to the end of the war – at an enormous cost in lives on both sides.

The German strategy to achieve a rapid victory, based on the Schlieffen Plan, had failed after initially coming close to success. Why? The reasons are complex and the subject of perennial discussion by military historians. One key factor is that the Plan was conceived solely as a military strategy and took little account of the political situation.

For example, Britain's role in a war between Germany and France was seen as marginal. When Schlieffen drew up his Plan, he took little account of the political repercussions in Britain of a German invasion

of Belgium. Also, the original Plan was drawn up before the full implications of the Anglo-French 'entente cordiale' of 1904 were realised, in particular the military talks between the two countries that were held a couple of years later. British commitment to the security of France was appreciably greater in 1914 than it had been when Schlieffen was poring over his railway timetables and road maps. Another important factor was that, contrary to Schlieffen's precept that war should not be fought on two fronts simultaneously, Germany attacked Russia in the east at the same time as it launched itself against France in the west. Germany's human and material resources were disastrously split between the two main arenas of war in Europe, the Western and Eastern Fronts.

* * *

The long twenty-five mile trek from the Fleurbaix sector to the Ypres Salient by G.O.M. and his comrades in the 1/6th Battalion of the West Yorkshires was accomplished by marching at night and resting during the day. After a stop at the village of Meteren, they set off again in the evening of Tuesday 29 June, 1915. G.O.M.'s sardonic comment was that it 'Rained like the deuce just after we started. Usual procedure. Got thoroughly wet and then "oil-sheets on". Curious institution, the British army. Have often wondered if German army carries on in the same way.' It seemed an interminable march. 'Kept on and on and on with occasional halts.' They crossed the border between France and Belgium and at 2 am the next morning, they arrived at Proven, a village some ten miles north-west of Ypres '. . . having been on the march from 6 pm. Had to practically carry E R [Ernest Ruffe] last 1/2 mile. Deuce of a march after three months' stagnation of trench life.'

Captain Tempest describes the march as one of the worst in the battalion's history. With fully loaded half-hundredweight packs and rifles, wearing sodden greatcoats, the men were marching in the dark and rain, slipping and floundering on the slimy cobbled roads:

> During the later stages of the march the frequently repeated cry throughout the Battalion was 'How far to Watou?' a town . . . just within the Belgian border. The answer invariably was 'two kilometres'. This question and answer had run many times up and down the weary column, when a wag, hearing the answer for the umpteenth time, at last shouted out, 'Thank God, we're keeping up with the damned place!'

However, the morning of Wednesday 30 June brought a pleasant surprise. On looking round, G.O.M. and his comrades '. . . found

ourselves in a beautiful country, with cornfields and hopfields. Every
available inch under cultivation. Visited the town of Proven. Found it
a jolly little place, practically stocked with English goods at English
prices. Had rather a good time (along with splendid weather) . . .'
There was also cheap, state-subsidised, locally grown Belgian tobacco
for sale in the shops.

The delights of Proven and its surrounding countryside proved to
be a short and highly deceptive interlude. On Sunday 4 July '. . . we
packed up again. We marched in boiling hot weather [into] Proven,
where we embarked on buses. This method of going up [to the front
line] is often spoken of but rarely seen.'

The buses set off on a ten miles journey '. . . through the town of
Poperinghe . . . En route we noticed the strong lines of defence. This
is the way to Calais which the Huns never travelled.' When they
arrived at Vlamertinghe, just west of Ypres, G.O.M. noted as they left
the buses that the church and surrounding houses had been battered.
The Battalion then marched off '. . . over very desolate looking
country [towards] the notorious Yser Canal . . .' where they '. . .
relieved a battalion of the Royal Irish Regiment who had been there
28 days.' They arrived at 11 at night and had their first taste of life
in the Ypres Salient when they were 'stood to' at 2 am the next
morning for an enemy attack that failed to materialise. Later that day,
G.O.M. wrote in his diary:

> This [Yser] Canal must have been a fine waterway in peace time. High
> banks on each side, lined with 60 foot trees in the French style. These
> banks were both honeycombed with dug-outs now, on the side furthest
> from the enemy. The weather . . . was fine. There was a punt on the
> canal which was pretty freely used and a good deal of swimming went
> on until it transpired that there were bodies in the canal. We were about
> a mile to the north of Ypres, which the Germans shelled every day both
> with heavy shrapnel and high explosive. The activity of aircraft and
> artillery was abnormal. The guns were going all day long. This is not
> to be wondered at, as the place absolutely reeks of artillery.

At this period in the Ypres Salient, there were no large scale, dramatic
battles, no great advances or retreats. It was, though, a time of
continuous intensive conflict, with all the dangers and weariness of
trench warfare, and a number of small-scale engagements. There were
some desultory and many fierce bombardments, which might last up
to three or four hours, or even longer. German shelling always seemed
more intensive than the British response. This is substantiated by

Captain Tempest, who comments on the shortage of shells at this time – there was rationing of just three shells per gun per day. An officer is cited as saying that 'Our shelling was like barking against thunder.'

In the intervals between artillery bombardments, movement in the trenches was severely restricted by bursts of enemy machine-gun fire and there was the ever-present danger of single, deadly sniper shots. The two front lines were mostly between 80 and 150 yards apart, though at one point this narrowed to just thirty yards. There was a steady trickle of casualties, dead and wounded.

There was little rest at night. Any real or imagined flurry of activity on the enemy's part precipitated the command 'stand to', at which those who were not already on sentry duty had to turn out of their dugouts and man the trenches. Both sides sent night patrols into No Man's Land and the sky would be lit up by flares. Captain Tempest comments:

> A night attack at Ypres was always an awe-inspiring sight – from a distance. The whole salient was lit up like a devil's smithy. Thousands of Verey lights [flares] of all colours, and the flames of bursting shells, drew a ring of fire round the City of Ypres, the ruins of the Cloth Hall – gaunt and naked in the glare of bursting shells – being clearly seen by our men from their shelters on the Canal bank.

Food was a major problem, as well as sleep. The Battalion historian again:

> Elaborate plans and arrangements for Soup Kitchens and hot food were made with the best of intentions at Divisional Headquarters, but, as was unfortunately often the case, failed to materialise in the front line system. In mud where it took an hour for a man to move a hundred yards, it can easily be imagined that no one would face the almost incredible exertion – let alone danger – of going back to reserve positions for hot soup or a cup of tea.

In *Death's Men* (1978), Denis Winter describes food as the prime comfort of the men in the trenches. A ration party would draw dry rations every day and bring them up to the front line:

> Dry rations would be put in sandbags. Tea and sugar would be put into separate corners and crudely tied in place. Tins of jam,[1] Maconochie stew and bully beef [corned beef] would be added with bread and mail on top. A label would indicate the trench section and there would be wet rations – stew and porridge – in screwtop containers strapped to

---

[1] I remember G.O.M. telling me that the tinned jam was always plum and apple.

men's backs. Men looked forward to an arrival, which would guarantee a breakfast of half a round of biscuit, a loaf between three, tin of butter between nine, tin of jam between six and half a mug of tea.

That, Denis Winter points out, was the theory. In practice, '. . . bearers might fall into shell holes, adding the flavour of chemicals, excrement and dead bodies as garnish'. Bully beef and biscuits made the soldiers so thirsty that the ration of half a mug of tea was totally inadequate. Yet, in spite of the hazards, 'Food was . . . always a hope and a joy, an improvisation and a scarcity, yet [even] at its worst it provided a moment of good memories and companionship in the trench routine.'

Feet and footwear were another preoccupation. 'Trench foot' was rife, caused by standing for long periods in freezing water. At one time, the battalion reported forty cases in two days. The condition was taken seriously: in bad cases it could lead to gangrene. One counter measure was the use of waterproof wellingtons or gumboots, in place of the normal lace-up leather ones. However, there were only enough gumboots for the battalion that was actually in the line. When the outgoing battalion was being relieved, the men took off their gumboots and laid them out in a pile for the incoming battalion. The description by Captain Tempest of what happened next could furnish a scenario for one of Charlie Chaplin's silent comedies:

> The incoming battalion then marched up in the darkness and each man changed into the first muddy gumboots he could find, being fortunate if he got a decent pair, and no odd numbers. The confusion . . . on a pitch dark night, with heavy rain, fields everywhere over the ankles in mud, and with frequent bursts of enemy shelling, may be left to the reader's imagination. Every effort was made to organise the distribution, but it was too complicated to work smoothly under bad conditions. More than one fellow marched to the line every relief night with a left boot on a right foot: or became stuck in the mud on the way up and had to leave his gumboots behind him, and finish the journey in his stockings.

Coming into this maelstrom of chaos and death, G.O.M.s' first impressions were of a well-developed system of defences, with trenches that were deeper and narrower than he and his pals had been used to further south in the Fleurbaix sector. However, not for the first time, appearances proved to be deceptive, especially when the rains came. The Regimental historian, Laurie Magnus, came to describe the defences as '. . . stinking trenches filled with human

wreckage', while the Battalion historian departs from his usual measured prose to sum up the conditions faced by G.O.M.'s 1/6th Battalion of the West Yorkshires in the Ypres Salient:

> So much misery, mud, murder was nowhere else compressed in so small a space. The ground reeked with gas: was polluted with dead and the debris of a hundred battles: was tortured by an everlasting storm of shells. There was no possibility of peace or safety in the Salient.

On Tuesday 6 July 1915, two days after the battalion's arrival, G.O.M. records that they were stood to in reserve lines near the canal from 5 am to 6.30 am. 'Attack made on small section of German line by RB. [Rifle Brigade] after a bombardment of half an hour. Successful. 200 yards taken.' Captain Tempest records that the advance was in fact about 500 yards and that three lines of German trenches were captured. G.O.M. says that just behind the front line things were;

> . . . fairly quiet except for an occasional short bombardment by the Huns. 'A' Company got more than we did. R [his younger brother, Rupert] and F came through all right. Bombarded for half an hour with gas shells once. Helmets necessary to protect the eyes. Gas said to be xylene di-bromide. Certainly organic.

It was G.O.M.'s first experience of gas warfare. It would not be his last.

Six days later, on Monday 12 July, the Germans counterattacked to try to retake the ground they had lost. G.O.M. describes a 'Fairly heavy bombardment. We stood to. Heard later that attack had been beaten off. After considerable delay, we marched off up to front line to relieve 5th WYR [their sister unit, 1/5th Battalion West Yorkshire Regiment] which we did about 12 pm.'

What surprised G.O.M. was that for the first time he found himself '. . . in an actual trench'. In the Fleurbaix sector, where the battalion had been before moving to the Ypres Salient, the water table was so high that it was not possible to dig deep trenches. They had lived and fought behind parapets built above ground level. By contrast:

> These trenches had been dug by the French and occupied by them. We were on the northerly side of the notorious Ypres Salient and could see the ruins of that town behind us. I believe we were near the village of St Julien. One curious point about the position of our platoon, we were in a section of trench . . . from where we were unable to see German lines at all.

This inability to see the enemy – or indeed anything of significance in the landscape forward from the front line – was a common feature of the war on the Western Front. In a letter to his mother written on 5 July 1916 (reproduced in *Winds of Change*), Harold Macmillan, then a subaltern in the Grenadier Guards, writes:

> Perhaps the most extraordinary thing about a modern battlefield is the desolation and emptiness of it all . . . One cannot emphasise this point too much. Nothing is to be seen of war or soldiers – only the split and shattered trees and the burst of an occasional shell reveal anything of the truth. One can look for miles and see no human being. But in those miles of country lurk (like moles or rats, it seems) thousands, even hundreds of thousands of men, planning against each other perpetually some new device of death. Never showing themselves, they launch at each other bullet, bomb, aerial torpedo and shell . . . And yet the landscape shows nothing of all this – nothing but a few shattered trees and 3 or 4 thin lines of earth and sandbags; these and the ruins of towns and villages are the only signs of war anywhere visible.

Life in the St Julien sector of the front line was especially dangerous. Just behind the German forward trench, no more than 250 yards away, there was a heavily fortified low rise in the ground, known as 'The High Command'. No more than ninety feet high, it nevertheless occupied a commanding position in the flat countryside. Enemy snipers were ideally positioned to make any movement in the British trenches very hazardous.

The Wednesday two days later was something of a low point. G.O.M. was in the front trench, with a German artillery barrage overhead, shelling the reserves immediately behind. As if that wasn't enough, it '. . . rained all night. Wet through once again. Rather fed up.' Translating G.O.M.'s lifelong understatement of his feelings, that last sentence may be interpreted as deep depression. Though he didn't know it at the time, the following day, Thursday 16 July, would be the end of a chapter in his military life. It would be his last day as a Private in 'C' Company of the 1/6th Battalion of the West Yorkshires, surrounded by the warm, familiar accents of his pals from the neighbouring streets of Bradford. His life as one of the hundreds of thousands of members of the PBI – Poor Bloody Infantry – would cease, though not his time in the trenches.

CHAPTER 5

Comical Chemical Corporals

A T 5 PM ON 22 APRIL 1915, near Langemark in the Ypres sector, soldiers of the French 45th (Algerian) and 87th (Territorial) Divisions looking towards the enemy lines saw a grey-green cloud forming above the German trenches. As a heavy artillery bombardment opened up, the sinister cloud rolled across no man's land, carried by a steady breeze from the north-east. Within minutes, thousands of French and French North African troops were choking, retching and gasping for breath, yellow froth foaming from their mouths and nostrils. They abandoned their trenches and struggled half-blinded to the rear, desperately trying to escape the gas that had enveloped them.

Following the gas cloud, German infantry in gas masks advanced over the now undefended allied trenches and within a couple of hours had opened up a breach four miles wide and two miles deep. The despatch sent to the War Office by Field Marshall Sir John French, Commander-in-Chief of the British forces, read:

> What followed is practically indescribable. The effect of the gas was so overwhelming that the whole of the positions occupied by the French Divisions was rendered incapable of any resistance. It was impossible at first to realise what had happened. Fumes and smoke obscured everything. Hundreds of men were thrown into a stupor, and after an hour the whole position had to be abandoned . . .

Then, although they had achieved an astonishing breakthrough and had a clear path ahead of them, the German troops came to a halt and began to dig in for the night. There were no reserves following them up and they feared getting overextended.

Soldiers of the First Canadian Division on the French right were also affected by the gas attack, which was on a massive scale. 160 tons of gas had been released from 5,700 cylinders by the German 35th Pioneer Regiment, a special gas unit under the leadership of Fritz Haber, who had pioneered research on gas at the Kaiser Wilhelm

43

Institute for Physical Chemistry and was later to receive the Nobel prize.[1]

When the allied troops realised that the gas was chlorine, defensive precautions were improvised. Pieces of cloth – socks, scarves, anything that came to hand – were soaked in water or urine, then tied over nose and mouth. In desperate haste, the Canadians regrouped to try to cover their open left flank. During the night, they even managed to mount a limited counterattack, misleading the Germans about their strength.

The following day, a scratch British force was rushed forward to help plug the worst gaps in the line. On the left, the remnants of the demoralised French troops mounted an inadequately prepared and supported counterattack that was beaten off by the Germans with heavy casualties.

At 4 am the next morning, 24 April, the Germans launched another fifteen-foot-high rolling cloud of gas against the hastily redrawn Canadian front line. The Canadians were heavily outnumbered: they had eight battalions of troops in defence against no fewer than twenty-four battalions of the German army. In a period of intensely bitter fighting, the Canadians held their ground and the German attackers were unable to break through.

One week later, there was a third German gas attack, at Hill 60 on the right (southern) flank of the Ypres sector. This time it was the Dorset Regiment that took the weight of the assault and held on, in spite of suffering huge casualties. These were the opening phases of 'Second Ypres', as the battle came to be known.

For a week, no news of the deployment of poison gas by the Germans – its first use on the Western Front – reached the British public. Then the London newspapers competed with each other in their denunciation of this 'atrocity', this 'cowardly form of warfare'. *The Times* thundered against the enemy's '. . . deliberate resort to this atrocious method of warfare . . . a diabolical contrivance.'

However, the widespread popular indignation about the advent of gas as a battlefield weapon did not impede Sir John French from launching two initiatives: first, the design and production of gas masks which would help front line soldiers to survive and fight

---

[1]Fritz Haber received the Nobel prize for chemistry in 1918, an award that was not without its critics in view of the part he had played in developing gas warfare. He resigned from his post as Director of the Kaiser Wilhelm Institute in 1933 in protest at the Nazi regime's anti-Jewish policies and accepted a post at Cambridge University: however, he died before he could take it up.

through gas attacks; and second, the preparation of retaliatory action, which would enable the British army to exploit the potential of gas as a weapon.

To carry forward the second initiative, Major C H Foulkes was given the task of recruiting and organising 'Special Companies' (later, the Special Brigade) of the Royal Engineers. The 40-year-old Foulkes was an all-round sportsman, whose many athletic accomplishments included captaincy of the Scottish hockey team in the 1908 Olympic Games. He had seen service in West and South Africa, the West Indies and Ceylon (now Sri Lanka). He had fought in 'First Ypres' in November 1914 and been awarded the Distinguished Service Order for rescuing a wounded man under heavy fire. As he freely admitted, he knew nothing whatsoever about chemistry or the use of gas in warfare, but he took great care from the outset to surround himself with those who did. Many of the chemists who formed the nucleus of this specialised branch of the Royal Engineers were recruited directly from university and college departments of chemistry, though others, like G.O.M., came from the ranks of the infantry.

* * *

G.O.M.'s diary records that after breakfast on Friday 16 July 1915, he received an order from the Company Sergeant Major to report immediately with full pack at Battalion Headquarters. There, he reported to the Adjutant and was told he was going for a course in gas and that he must report to Brigade Headquarters. He hung about until dark and was then ordered to set off in a horse-drawn wagon back towards the West Yorkshire transport lines. Halfway there, he was '. . . thrown out through horses running into ditch trying to pass a lorry.' However, he eventually arrived safely and fell asleep in the back of the wagon.

The next morning, after 'a deuced fine breakfast', he set off on one of those interminable, complicated journeys which have afflicted the lives of fighting soldiers for two thousand years and more. First, he marched to an Army Service Corps depot near Poperinghe, about eight miles west of Ypres. Then, continuing west, he was taken by lorry through Steenvorde to Cassel, some twelve miles away. At this railhead, he was told to catch a train for the seven-mile hop south to Hazebrouck. Then, after a wait that gave him time to look round the small town, he caught another train going west.

The phrase 'catching a train' might give the impression of sitting back in upholstered comfort, watching the Flemish countryside roll by. It was not quite like that. The trains consisted of cattle trucks.

Seating – if you were lucky – was on the boarded floor. In this case, G.O.M., along with his friend Rob and a handful of others from the West Yorkshires, was bundled out of the sliding doors of the cattle truck while the train passed through Wizernes station without stopping. Picking up their rifles and half-hundredweight packs, the group who had 'been volunteered' were marched off to the village of Helfaut, the depot of the newly formed Special Companies of the Royal Engineers.

The site had been carefully chosen by Major Foulkes. It was about four miles south of the British GHQ at St Omer, near enough for him to have ready access to the centre of decision-making, but not so close that he would have his arrangements readily interfered with from higher up the chain of command. Very soon, G.O.M.

> . . . learned what we were here for. The War Office had determined to form a gas-corps; we had finished with the infantry & were now full-fledged Royal Engineers, with promotion to Corporal. This is the end of my life in the infantry, which had been a hard one while it lasted. My only regret was that I had left a lot of good pals, whom I had worked and lived with for nearly 12 months & that I had to leave my brother there.

The written diary is not quite as I remember my father telling the story. His oral version was that, at morning parade on Friday 16 July, the Company Sergeant Major had barked out 'Anybody who knows anything about chemistry, two paces step forward . . . MARCH!!' Before the war, G.O.M. had studied dyestuffs technology at Bradford Technical College, so, transgressing the age-old counsel of the private soldier that you should never put yourself forward as a volunteer for *anything*, he had stepped forward.

However, there was an immediate reward. The Royal Engineers Special Companies were unique in the British Army in that they contained no soldiers with the basic rank of private or its equivalent. The lowest rank was corporal – indeed, they were known as the 'Comical Chemical Corporals'.[2] Promotion from private to corporal brought a pay increase from one shilling (5p) a day – which with various special allowances could be ratcheted up to one shilling and ninepence (c 9p) – to three shillings (15p) a day: comparative riches.

G.O.M. writes proudly that he and his friend Rob were on '. . . the first guard in the Army composed entirely of full Corporals.'

---

[2] In *My Early Life* (1930), Winston Churchill referred to them as 'chemists in spectacles'.

Moreover, they weren't issued with rifles, but with .45 Webley revolvers. This was for two reasons – to give them a practical badge of authority (commissioned officers also had revolvers) and to avoid cumbersome rifles getting in the way when gas cylinders were being manoeuvred (see illus. 8).

G.O.M's group were among the first arrivals at the new 'gas' base at Helfaut, along with two batches direct from Britain. Along with his friend Rob, he was allocated to No 2 Section, 186th Company. Although his view of Helfaut was that it was 'only a potty little place', G.O.M. found life there very acceptable by contrast with the continuous shelling, machine-gun fire and sniping in the front line he had just left.

In his memoir *With the Special Brigade RE*, one of G.O.M.'s colleagues, Martin S ('Syd') Fox describes Helfaut as:

> . . . a pleasant village on the edge of a large common . . . It possessed a tall stone obelisk called the Duke of Orleans's monument, marking the spot from which Napoleon reviewed his troops before Waterloo. Nearby was a windmill for the grinding of corn, and one could obtain the French 'cartwheel' loaves from the house attached; there was a modern type of school, and two or three estaminets; the church stood a little apart from the houses; all the inhabitants were very friendly . . . Our billets were barns, and tents in the adjoining fields . . .

However, not much had happened by the time G.O.M. arrived: 'The whole business seemed to be in a very embryonic condition, nobody knowing exactly what was going to happen. The main idea at present seemed to be to get some trenches dug on a fairly extensive common adjoining the village.' On his first full day – Sunday 18 July – he spent from 9 am until 12 noon and from 2 pm until 3.30 pm digging trenches in the boiling sun.

Later that afternoon a draft of academic chemists, recruited from the chemistry departments of universities and colleges, arrived directly from England. They did not get a very sympathetic welcome from G.O.M. and the other battle-hardened ex-infantrymen who had been fighting in the front line. G.O.M.'s comment was that they were a:

> . . . studious-looking lot. Turned out they thought they were coming out here for the purpose of laboratory work & were highly indignant because they found out that their work for some time would consist of trench digging. Lots of talk of 'enlisted under false pretences', 'questions asked in Parliament' etc. Got little sympathy from Rob and I, who

considered they were deuced lucky, and ought to have been in the army long ago.

Time and further acquaintance led to G.O.M. softening his attitude towards the unblooded newcomers: 'Some of the specially enlisted men were very decent chaps, including Heasman, Sutcliffe, Hall, Hoadley and a few more.' According to Donald Richter in *Chemical Soldiers* (1994), about half the personnel at Helfaut (but not G.O.M., whose knowledge of chemistry had been acquired at a technical college course) had university degrees. Many were considerably over-qualified for the work they were supposed to do. D A Clibbens had a BSc from London, an MSc from Bristol and a PhD from Jena and Freiburg Universities in Germany. His section officer thought that Clibbens and three similar academic high-flyers were not suited to fighting duties, so he put them on sanitary fatigues, scrubbing out the latrines with their brooms. In their time off, the four 'bog wallahs' organised classes for the village children. Writing over half a century later in the *Special Brigade Newsletter* (no 20, July 1968), Clibbens commented wryly on the confusion that there was about the qualifications needed to become a gas Special:

> ... if you told the recruiting officer in 1914 that you were a chemist, he automatically put you in the Royal Army Medical Corps, believing you to be a pharmacist. A year later, if you told him you were a pharmacist he pushed you into the Special Brigade, believing you to be a chemist.

At this time, life was not especially hard at the Helfaut base. In G.O.M.'s words: 'We led a very placid and easy life; a very quiet one indeed, which was a pleasant change. Had cricket and football matches on the common. Weather very decent the whole time.' As well as digging trenches on the common, the men of the newly formed Special Companies were engaged in squad drill, route marches and target practice with their revolvers. Above all, they got used to working with gas cylinders – although the use of the word 'gas' and 'cylinder' were prohibited for security reasons. A cylinder was officially known as an 'accessory', though more colloquially as an 'oojah' or a 'roger'. There was a good deal of self-mockery:

> We are Fred Karno's army, the Roger Corps, RE,
> We cannot march,
> We cannot fight,
> What bloody good are we?

The development of gas as an offensive weapon had been given high priority by the War Office following the German gas attack at the end of April. In the account he wrote in 1934 of the work of the Special Brigade, *Gas!*, Major Foulkes described the first large scale experiment held near the Castner-Kellner chemical works at Runcorn, Cheshire, on 4 June 1915, by the side of the Manchester Ship Canal. The experiment was judged a great success. The clouds of chlorine gas released were so noxious that '. . . the bargees sailing past shouted abuse at us.' Nevertheless, the delivery of gas cylinders ran behind schedule and the supply of flexible connecting pipes became so problematic that iron ones with right angle bends had to be substituted.

In spite of these difficulties, Major Foulkes was able to stage a live demonstration of a gas attack on 22 August, barely five weeks after the first contingents had arrived at Helfaut. This was attended by Field Marshall Haig and twenty or thirty senior generals of the British First Army. Haig was very impressed – perhaps too impressed, as he began to envisage large scale gas attacks as the cornerstone of offensive warfare.

As summer turned into autumn, G.O.M. recorded that '. . . rumours began to fly about that we were going up the line.' On 3 September, to his intense annoyance, he was transferred from No 2 Section, 186th Company to No 28 Section, 188th Company (at this time, there were four gas Special Companies, numbered 186 to 189). He was 'very disgusted' at having to break with his new-found friends and 'interviewed a lot of people in authority' to no avail. To make matters worse, it poured with rain all day and they were turned out in the wet to hear a morale-boosting address by Major Foulkes.

The following day, the rumours turned out to be true. When they went on morning parade, they were issued with distinctive coloured brassards. They were ordered to wear these pink, white and green armbands – reminiscent of Neapolitan ice cream – so that, after launching a gas attack, they would avoid charges of desertion or malingering as they stayed with their empty gas cylinders in the trenches, while the infantry vanished through the smoke towards the German front line. Colonel Ernest Gold, a meteorologist who had been brought in by General Haig to coordinate intelligence on wind speed and direction, records in the *Special Brigade Newsletter* (no 41, May 1977) that before departure there was a short speech by company commander, Captain Percy-Smith, a former officer in the Deccan Horse, an Indian cavalry regiment, and known to all as 'By

God Percy' from his habit of prefacing every remark with 'By God
...' This proved to be in the best playing-fields-of-Eton tradition:

> Boys, you are going to take part in the greatest battle the army has yet
> prepared for. Advance is now at a standstill and the artillery and
> infantry are waiting for you to clear a way. Good luck to you all. Stick
> to your job whatever happens.

At 10 am on 4 September, a convoy of 68 London buses and eight
lorries left the base at Helfaut heading east towards the front line.
After a couple of hours or so they reached Béthune, where they got
out of the buses and were marched straight to the barracks in which,
according to G.O.M., they were 'incarcerated' until 4 pm, when they
were formed up and marched off again, finally reaching a bunch of
lorries. Getting on board, they set off once again – as so often in the
army, 'destination unknown'. Finally, at 7.30 pm, they reached the
village of Busnes, near Lillers, and 'after the usual messing around'
were put in a 'pretty decent' billet.

Busnes was about eight miles behind the front line and still
relatively untouched by the war. As a village, G.O.M. thought it was
'... quite a pretty one, with the usual big church, fairly good shops
and decent country round, although very flat.' Nothing much
happened in the next ten days or so, but G.O.M. 'Struck a very nice
little farm where Rob and I had feeds every night with a few of the
boys ...' Their pay rise was clearly coming in handy, but all were
only too aware that 'The life here ... was too good to last.'

CHAPTER 6

'Gas, GAS! Quick, Boys!'

THE GOOD LIFE AT BUSNES was brought to an abrupt end on Friday 17 September, when the Special Companies were swept up in the preparations for a major Allied offensive. This was the brainchild of Marshal Joffre, commander-in-chief of the French armies and hero of the battle of the Marne the previous autumn, when Paris had been saved. By the summer of 1915, the parallel lines of trenches on the Western front were beginning to take on an ominously permanent look, and the Allied high command was searching for a way to penetrate the German defences and break through to the open, undefended country beyond. Joffre's plan was to launch a twin offensive. British and French forces would attack on the Arras-Lens-la Bassée sector of the front, while further south there would be a French assault in the Champagne region, with various other diversionary sorties elsewhere to prevent the Germans from drawing off reserves to resist the Allies' main thrusts.

The British sector focused on Loos, just north-west of the industrial town of Lens. The open terrain sloped very gently upwards towards the German lines. There was little natural cover for advancing British troops. Ahead of them lay the remnants of heavily shelled mine workings, pitheads with towers and winding gear (*fosse*), slag heaps of mine waste (*crassier*) and ruined rows of miners' cottages. All had been fortified by the Germans, who found plenty of cover for machine-gun nests and high points for observation posts. It was no wonder that Lt Gen Sir Henry Rawlinson, Commander of IV Corps in the 1st Army, when inspecting the area in the summer of 1915, described it as '. . . most unfavourable ground.'

Surprise was not part of the plan. The offensive had been originally timed for earlier in September but was postponed until the 25th to allow the French to complete their preparations. A week before it eventually took place, the French ambassador in London reported that it was the subject of general gossip. The infantry assault was to be preceded by an intensive artillery bombardment to destroy the defensive positions and intimidate the German infantry and – a first

time for the Allies – gas would be launched on a massive scale to disable those German soldiers who had survived the shelling.

* * *

The Special Companies began their move up to the front on 17 September 1915, a burning hot day. Packed into three-ton lorries, G.O.M. and his comrades were driven south-east from the demi-paradise of Busnes to the village of Philosophe, near the main road from Béthune to Lens and just behind the front line. G.O.M. was not impressed:

> This had evidently been a mining village and a more dingy-looking hole I have seldom seen. Still a few frowsy-looking inhabitants knocking about. After a short march we reached the small town of Vermelles. There our section were billeted in an end cottage of a row facing the enemy lines. I have seen a good number of ruined towns in my time, but nothing to beat Vermelles. I have never seen a job more thoroughly carried out. There was scarcely a house standing in the place. I believe the place was retaken by the French in October 1914. A fine example of the efficiency of the French 75s and 'marmites' [artillery]. The curious thing about the whole business is the fact that the place Philosophe about half a mile away is practically untouched.

The next day, Saturday 18 September, they went up long communi-cation trenches nicknamed Gordon Alley and Border Lane to the front line. Each man carried a full petrol can of solution weighing 30 pounds as well as a 56-pound pack. A new front line had been dug, just 300 yards away from the Germans. At intervals, emplacements – disguised as fire steps – had been dug for the gas cylinders that were to feature in the attack. Each emplacement was designed to hold twelve cylinders.

Detailed organisational planning and immense human effort were involved in getting more than 5,000 gas cylinders, weighing some 300 tons, up to the front line. After being filled with chlorine gas at the Castner-Kellner factory at Runcorn in Cheshire, the cylinders were shipped by boat to Boulogne. There, they were transferred to a train for the 25-mile journey to a special storage depot at Audruick. From Audruick, the cylinders were taken up to the front line in three stages. First, they were taken by train to a railhead near Béthune, where soldiers from the Special Companies took the cylinders out of their boxes, loosened the dome caps which protected the gas valves, and then put the cylinders back in their boxes, refastening the box lids with a single screw.

Next, batches of cylinders were taken in horse-drawn wagons from the railhead to various local dumps positioned at intervals behind the front line. Finally, the cylinders were taken at night by parties of soldiers from the dumps to the front-line emplacements. Each full cylinder weighed at least 120 pounds – 60 pounds for the cylinder itself and 60 pounds gas – and was carried by poles or ropes slung through two carrying handles. Two men carried each six-foot-long cylinder up the saw-tooth shaped communications trenches, taking care to keep below the parapet so that they were not seen by the enemy. They stumbled along in the dark without any light.

In principle, nearby infantry were supposed to be requisitioned for these carrying duties, but this frequently failed to work in practice. Hard-pressed infantry officers understandably didn't want their men exhausted by 'coolie duty' of this kind. Indeed, they did not know what was in the long boxes marked 'accessory'. G.O.M. notes that he could sympathise with the infantry; when he had been in the West Yorkshires, he had often had to do similar carrying jobs for the Royal Engineers. Even though on this occasion the infantry fatigue parties did their job bringing up the cylinders and equipment, G.O.M. was up until three in the morning for the next few nights organising his emplacement, with its twelve cylinders and other equipment. When he was able to snatch an hour or two's sleep, it was in a trench or dugout.

Thursday 23 September was a long and arduous day. It started back at the chicory factory forward base at Gorre, near Béthune, with many hours spent examining and tying up the iron connecting pipes and parapet discharge pipes. In the evening, G.O.M and his friend Rob set off towards the front in a horse-drawn wagon with all the cumbersome apparatus. They travelled to their forward dump through heavy thunderstorms and pouring rain. Unloading the pipes, spanners and nuts and bolts, they set off on foot with other comrades – in G.O.M.'s words 'after the usual confusion' – at 9 pm. Their heavily laden trek took four hours. For G.O.M. it was

> ... a terrible journey. The pipes (some ten feet long) were very awkward round the traverses, and the trench itself was muddy and as the district was chalky we were all over the place. We arrived, nearly all of us in a very exhausted condition, about 1 am ...

The following morning, Friday 24 September, was spent preparing the emplacement for the attack, while the rain continued. Some trenches were one or two feet deep in water. There were two engineers to each emplacement and G.O.M.'s partner was:

... Griffiths whom I knew at the Technological College and came from the 'Bradford Pals' (16th West Yorkshires). After we had got everything fixed up to our mutual satisfaction, we went back to our dugout. During the course of the day, I watched the bombardment of the German front line from a very favourable position. Our heavy and field artillery were blasting their barbed wire and front line off the face of the earth. It was a fine but terrible sight, the accuracy of our fire being remarkable. This has been going on for three days! Stopped for the night in our emplacement.

Six infantry divisions were in place to attack across a front six miles wide, with a further three divisions in reserve to follow through the assault once the German lines had been broken. In the front line, there were nearly 1,500 officers and men of the Special Companies ready to discharge 5,500 gas cylinders and countless smoke candles. G.O.M.'s emplacement was virtually in the centre of the British line of attack, just north of the Vermelles-Hulluch road.

That night, with the artillery bombardment apparently successful and everything set for a dawn attack, indecision and uncertainty prevailed at General Haig's headquarters. Early on, the hourly meteorological reports showed a slight bias towards a favourable wind speed and direction, but the wind speed was dropping as the night went on and the direction became variable.

One of the Special Companies' officers, J W Sewill, writing in the *Special Brigade Newsletter* (no 7, April 1962), said that just one hour before zero hour the wind had dropped to practically nil, with continuing drizzle making the conditions unfavourable. He telephoned Brigade Headquarters to say that conditions were so unfavourable that he would not hold himself responsible for the effect of the gas on British troops. He was given the order to carry on as planned. Finally, the decision was taken that the gas should be turned on at 5.50 am and that the infantry should go over the top at 6.30 am.

The timetable for the crucial forty minutes of gas and smoke discharge is set out in the written orders preserved by Colonel Ernest Gold (reproduced in *Special Brigade Newsletter* no 41, May 1977):

0	Start the gas and run six cylinders one after the other at full blast until all are exhausted.
0.10–0.12	Start the smoke. The smoke is to run concurrently with the gas if the gas is not exhausted by 0.12.
0.20	Start the gas again and run six cylinders one after the other at full blast until all are exhausted.

0.32–0.40	Start the smoke again. The smoke is to run concurrently with the gas if the gas is not exhausted by 0.32.
0.38	Turn all gas off punctually. Thicken up smoke with triple candles. Prepare for assault.
0.40	ASSAULT.

The simple phrases 'start' and 'turn off' the gas conceal a frenzy of activity with spanners, nuts, valves, connecting and discharge pipes, mixed in with lighting smoke candles – all carried out wearing gas helmets with limited visibility. Inevitably, there were many leakages of gas. G.O.M's diary gives a graphic account of the first day of the Battle of Loos, as seen by a corporal in the RE Special Companies, one of those responsible for launching the British Army's first gas attack:

The day [Saturday, 25 September, 1915] broke dull and a slight breeze was falling. The wind was blowing about a quarter left from us at about 5 mph. The South Staffordshire Regiment (7th Division) was occupying our part of the line. We received our orders and zero times fairly early on. Zero was 5.50 am. We started our performance on the minute. I got a big mouthful [of gas] with the first cylinder and then, *of course*, pulled my helmet down. We had only two pipes for twelve cylinders and had to change over when one was empty. The rotten apparatus they had given us was leaking all over the place and we were working in a cloud of gas. We sweated ourselves to death and only got eight cylinders off.

G.O.M.'s experience of the faulty equipment and chaotic conditions is echoed in the diary kept by R B Purves, also a member of 'M' company, published in the *Special Brigade Newsletter* (no 6, February 1962):

Leaks of chlorine came out at the joints, but after some struggle, got things going … went at it as best I could, choking, coughing, half-blinded, and feeling as if last moments had come. It's impossible to put any of the sensations on paper; but I shall not forget it … A hail of shells, both British and German, were landing all around, and a rattle of machine guns was everywhere … our smoke helmets were practically useless.

Syd Fox of 'C' Company tells a similar story in his *History of the Special Brigade RE*:

… in those unfortunate areas where the released gas was blown back into our own lines, the cylinders were quickly turned off, though too late to avoid gas entering portions of our front line; serious casualties

were caused among the infantry assembled there, as well as among our own Companies.

After forty minutes of this turmoil, G.O.M.'s diary records:

> All gas had to be turned off at 6.28 am. At 6.30 the infantry had to go over the parapet. We finished on time. The Staffordshires [1st Bn South Staffordshire Regiment, 7th Division] went over where we were as if they were on parade, at the slope and by the right. There was very little rifle fire but it was an inspiring sight. Pretty soon the German artillery opened up. Their fire wasn't particularly heavy, but they were sending over some heavy stuff and I had a few near squeaks.

In fact, advancing through the clouds of gas and smoke generated by G.O.M. and his colleagues in the RE Special Companies, the infantry were taking heavy losses, especially from German machine-gun fire (see illus. 10). The 1st Bn South Staffordshires, whose discipline G.O.M. had so much admired, suffered 448 casualties in the attack.

Some were luckier than others. One infantryman who escaped was G.O.M.'s Bradford neighbour, the future playwright and man of letters, J B Priestley. Crouching in a reserve trench behind the front line, Priestley awaited the command to move forward and join the attack. Luckily for him it was a call that never came – the momentum of the assault had petered out.

Priestley was not the only literary figure to survive the Battle of Loos. A mile or so to G.O.M.'s left, the 20-year-old Robert Graves commanded a company of the Welch Fusiliers. Fourteen years later, his fictionalised account of the chaos and confusion of the Battle of Loos in *Goodbye to All That* (1929) contributed to the book's reputation as one of the notable anti-war tracts of the period between the two world wars.

Many personal accounts by infantrymen and others have been gathered together in Philip Warner's *The Battle of Loos* (1976). However, one of the most vivid descriptions of what was, literally, the fog of war during this vicious battle is a letter sent home by an unnamed infantry officer, whose unit is not specified, writing home from a hospital bed in le Touquet just two days after the assault (*Special Brigade Newsletter* no 41, May 1977). After the gas and smoke discharge launched by G.O.M. and his comrades ceased:

> . . . I got over the parapet and from this point the tragedy began . . . At the time the gas cloud was being released, the wind was blowing at the rate of only 2 mph. As our front faced south-east this meant that the gas travelled 'half right' from our front. The gas rolled out of the

cylinders in dense sickly-looking yellow clouds and seemed to pile up after a time instead of going forward . . .

We started on our way but soon realised that we did not know where we were going. The gas hung in a thick pall over everything and it was impossible to see more than ten yards and everyone scattered. I went on, thinking I knew the way. Others were running or walking in the direction of the German line. They looked like ghosts because of the smoke helmets they wore. I was stifled in my helmet and I looked for a way through the ditches and shell-holes by peering through the rectangular mica window in the helmet. I passed men gassed and dying and I shall never forget the sight to my dying day.

I crept blindly forward, a bomb in one hand and holding my helmet tightly round my neck with the other. Then I came across some of my men lying in a row, waiting for the gas to clear before going forward. I joined them and found the air more breathable so took my helmet off – an unspeakable relief!

We went forward and got to the German wire, only to find it intact. It was evident that the Germans were holding that part very strongly so it would have been madness to attempt to rush it with only about ten men. We crawled on until a parapet loomed in front.

The gas and smoke was still thick. I came to a ditch about three feet deep and found a dozen wounded men in it. I gave them water and was able to direct them to the British lines . . . A few minutes later, I was hit in the thigh. I ripped up my breeches to apply a field dressing and, almost at the same time, the smoke cleared and I found myself a target for both sides, so I lay still.

I had to lie there, wounded and on the wet ground for twelve hours until it was dark. The Germans continued to shell our position and the noise was nerve-racking. It started raining later and eventually I left all my equipment and crawled VERY slowly to a ditch near some trees and so made my way back to our own lines, the dressing station, a hospital train and, finally, to the hospital at le Touquet.

Not long after the start of the infantry assault, casualties started streaming back towards the members of the Special Companies in their gas emplacements. In G.O.M.'s words:

Soon the wounded began to come back and we saw some horrible wounds and bandaged up a good number. All at once a number of men (unwounded) came back with a tale that they hadn't been able to get through the barbed wire. My opinion was that they had 'got the wind up'. Soon an order came 'Every man stand to – German counter attack!' My feelings can be imagined, but it was only a rumour! The only Germans coming over were prisoners under escort. There were a few young lads among them, but the majority looked no different in age and

appearance to our lads. A goodly number looked as if they had suffered from our little effort. About 11 Griffiths and I decided to push off, as we could do no further good by staying. I was in a very exhausted condition, couldn't breathe properly and had a deuce of a headache.

By this time, G.O.M. saw growing evidence of the number of casualties suffered in the initial assault:

Going down the communication trench and across the fields near Vermelles were streams of wounded of all descriptions, a sight I don't want to see again but will have to, I'm afraid. We were a terrible time getting down the trench owing to the wounded, especially a badly wounded sergeant on a stretcher: a chaplain was acting as stretcher bearer. The Huns were sending over occasional shrapnel and just after we got out of the trench, over came some 5.9 inch shells. We got back. I was absolutely done when we reached the village and fell out. Griffiths went on and brought back one of our lot to give a hand with my equipment etc. We joined up just before the company moved off and then we had the deuce of a march back to the chicory factory [the Special Companies' forward base near Béthune]. After having something to eat and drink, got down to it and slept until Sunday 26 September.

So ended, for a fortunate survivor, the first day of the Battle of Loos.

Dulce et Decorum Est

Bent double, like old beggars under sacks,
Knock-kneed, coughing like hags, we cursed through sludge,
Till on the haunting flares we turned our backs
And towards our distant rest began to trudge.
Men marched asleep. Many had lost their boots
But limped on, blood-shod. All went lame; all blind;
Drunk with fatigue; deaf even to the hoots
Of tired, outstripped Five-Nines that dropped behind.

Gas! GAS! Quick, boys! – An ecstasy of fumbling,
Fitting the clumsy helmets just in time;
But someone still was yelling out and stumbling,
And flound'ring like a man in fire or lime . . .
Dim, through the misty panes and thick green light,
As under a green sea, I saw him drowning.
In all my dreams, before my helpless sight,
He plunges at me, guttering, choking, drowning.

If in some smothering dreams you too could pace
Behind the wagon that we flung him in,
And watch the white eyes writhing in his face,
His hanging face, like a devil's sick of sin;
If you could hear, at every jolt, the blood
Come gargling from the froth-corrupted lungs,
Obscene as cancer, bitter as the cud
Of vile, incurable sores on innocent tongues,
My friend, you would not tell with such high zest
To children ardent for some desperate glory,
The old Lie: Dulce et decorum est
Pro patria mori.[1]

    Wilfred Owen

(killed in action on the Sambre & Oise Canal on 4 November 1918,
one week before the Armistice)

---

[1]There is no greater honour than to die for one's country.

CHAPTER 7

Three More Years and Then . . .

F OR G.O.M. AND HIS BROTHERS-IN-ARMS in the gas Special Companies, 25 September 1915 marked their engagement in the
opening assault of the Battle of Loos. They had done their job in
launching the chlorine gas and smoke that lay in a dense cloud over
the battlefield. They had taken casualties: one in every seven had been
killed or wounded from enemy shelling and machine-gun fire, even
though none had ever left the front line trenches.

The fiercest fighting at Loos continued until 28 September. Among
the reinforcements was the newly formed Guards Division, which was
ordered to attack Hill 70 on 27 September. Hill 70 had previously
been captured by the British on the opening day of the battle, only to
be recaptured by the Germans the following day. Harold Macmillan
records in *Winds of Change* that, as they moved up to the front line
under heavy artillery fire:

> What was distressing for our men was that the whole ground we
> covered in our march was filled, or seemed to be filled, with the
> remnants of troops who had attacked in the earlier days of the battle
> . . . Some were dead, some wounded, some broken and having lost all
> discipline or order. I have often wondered since why the decision was
> made to put in these divisions, who had never seen a shot fired and
> come straight from England, ahead of the Guards Division. It seemed
> a fatal error.

Ordered to retake Hill 70, Macmillan's Grenadier Guards battalion
advanced under heavy fire, with little idea of what was happening on
their flanks:

> Of the meaning of all this, while it was going on, I had of course the
> dimmest idea. All that I knew was that we were advancing to attack in
> the conventional open-order formation, under considerable fire from
> shells and bullets. At the time, however, one does not notice these
> things. There is a kind of daze that makes one impervious to emotion.
> Anyway, it was my first experience of a battle, and I could not suppose
> that this was any worse than usual.

In fact, Macmillan was concussed by a head wound and received a
bullet through his right hand. Dazed and semi-conscious, he was

evacuated to hospital in England: 'So ended my first battle. It was one in which, at any rate, I learnt the lesson of what was meant by the phrase "the fog of war".'[1]

The battle stuttered on for another two weeks or so with smaller scale attacks and counterattacks. Initially, the British assault had gained some ground in the centre, though never achieving the hoped for breakthrough. At the end, the front lines settled a mile or so at most to the east of their original position, across a two-mile width. The German second line trenches were never reached.

There were over 60,000 British solders dead, wounded, taken prisoner of war and missing. Some units were virtually wiped out. Of the nineteen officers of 6th Bn King's Own Scottish Borderers, twelve were killed and the remaining seven wounded: all but one of its non-commissioned officers (sergeants and corporals) were cut down and over 600 privates. Just to the left of G.O.M.'s position, 70 per cent of the 2nd Bn Royal Warwickshire Regiment were mowed down before reaching the enemy front line. A little to the north, it was a similar story with the 5th Bn Cameron Highlanders: out of 800 officers and men, only two officers and seventy men were left standing at the end of the day. It is difficult to make a precise comparison with German losses, as they were recorded on a different basis, but they may have been at half the British level, or slightly higher. It is hard to argue with Niall Cherry's conclusion in his comprehensive account of the battle in *Most Unfavourable Ground* (2005) that for the Allies Loos '. . . achieved nothing of any material gain except work for the medical services.'

What part did gas play in the outcome of the Battle of Loos? It was by some way the largest scale use of gas throughout the whole of the First World War. The Allied High Command had hoped that it would play a decisive role in enabling our troops to break through the German lines. It did not, though it undoubtedly weakened the German defence. However, because of the poor weather conditions, the massive gas discharge caused death and distress to some of the British attackers as well as to the German defenders: even three of

---

[1]After convalescence, Harold Macmillan returned to active service in France. The following year, he fought in the Battle of the Somme. He was hit in the left thigh by a burst of machine-gun fire and the bullets lodged in his pelvis. Before being rescued, he lay dazed and semi-conscious in a shell hole for twelve hours, feigning death so as not to attract the German soldiers who were all around. Brought back to hospital in England, he nearly died before his slow and intermittent recovery. His wounds were not finally healed until 1920, four years later, though his right hand never regained its full strength.

G.O.M.'s own mates in the Special Companies were killed by the gas they were discharging. Writing in *The Poisonous Cloud* (1968), Ludwig Haber, the son of Hans Haber, the German chemist who had pioneered the use of poison gas in warfare, reaches the conclusion that:

> Gas had failed at Loos. The first aim, retaliation, had been replaced by the more ambitious one – to save manpower and shells by forcing the enemy line with gas. On looking back, it is obvious that this was expecting too much of the chlorine cloud. The disappointment was all the greater because of the excessive optimism before the battle.

The evidence of G.O.M's diary, the individual accounts in Philip Warner's *The Battle of Loos* and the postwar contributions of survivors to the Royal Engineers Special Brigade Newsletters is that the Battle of Loos was the overwhelming, pivotal experience in the lives of those who were fortunate enough to survive. In Ludwig Haber's words 'No one who experienced gas forgot it – it may not have harmed their bodies, but it left an indelible stain on their minds.'

More than ninety years on, it has started to haunt me, the son of one of those survivors. G.O.M. was not the kind of man who constantly subjected his family and friends to tales of his terrible experiences during the war. In fact, I can't remember him ever talking about the Battle of Loos and the horrors of that day. But he bequeathed his war diary to me and it is on reading and re-reading it that I have begun to realise that 25 September 1915 was the day that G.O.M. could never forget – but it was also the day he was determined should not dominate the rest of his life. For my part, I am only thankful that I have not had to face the kind of test that my father passed with such unassuming heroism.

* * *

G.O.M.'s detailed diary finishes at the end of the first day of the Battle of Loos, the first and last occasion on which the British used gas as one of the main components in a major offensive. In the three years of trench warfare that followed, gas was used on many occasions, but in a limited, tactical way, to support more local attacks. This was because, in spite of the continuing enthusiasm of the head of the Special Brigade, Major Foulkes, there was a realisation in senior ranks that gas was subject to the vagaries of the weather and uncertain in its effects on British as well as enemy troops. It could not be relied on in a large scale offensive that had to be planned weeks or months in advance.

In the absence of a detailed diary for the period following 25 September 1915, G.O.M.'s summary notes on the list of places in which he served give some clue as to what happened to him subsequently. Eighteen days after the first day of the Battle of Loos, on 13 October, G.O.M. was back in action at Cambrin, a mile or so north of where he had been in the front line. It was a smaller scale offensive, aimed at capturing a heavily fought over strongpoint known as the Hohenzollern redoubt, which had been briefly in British hands during the Battle of Loos, and the nearby ruined mining village of Hulluch. The British line had been reinforced early that morning by the 46th Division, freshly arrived from the Ypres sector. However, these troops and their commanders were unfamiliar with the terrain round Loos. Indeed, the whole assault seems to have been quite pointless. The objectives were similar to those of the initial attack just over a fortnight earlier, but fewer soldiers were being used – and, yet again, there was no element of surprise. The British attempt to advance was yet again expected by the German machine gunners, who had been carefully positioned so that they had a clear field of fire across the No Man's Land between the opposing front line trenches.

In the morning, the wind was not favourable for launching gas. However, it changed during the course of a bright day and on this occasion, learning from the bitter experience of Loos, Field Marshall Haig had allowed for a flexible zero hour. An intensive British and French artillery barrage opened up at noon. One hour later, at 1 pm, G.O.M. and the other 'Specials' turned on their valves. It took an hour to discharge the 1,100 cylinders of gas. The white cloud of gas glided over towards the enemy lines just as it was supposed to do, with the infantry following behind. However, the Germans made a quick recovery from the gas attack. The British infantry came under heavy artillery, machine-gun and rifle fire, were unable to break through and withdrew. Casualties were very heavy. The 5th Bn North Staffordshires lost twenty officers, including their Commanding Officer, and 485 men in the first few minutes of the attack. The 6th Bn South Staffordshires lost eighteen officers and 456 men, leaving just four officers and 246 men standing at the end of the day (see illus. 12).

According to Syd Fox, G.O.M.'s 'C' Company comrade, in his memoir *With the Special Brigade RE*, this engagement was a testing time for all the gas Specials, as they were heavily bombarded by German artillery and '. . . experienced our first dose of lachrymatory shells, which came over in a deluge, and caused much inconvenience'. This is a masterpiece of understatement. The Specials suffered

heavily, considering that they had never left their trenches. Three of them were killed and eighteen wounded. Seventeen were gassed by leakages from their own cylinders. G.O.M.'s company commander, Lt D M Wilson (whom I met at my father's funeral some fifty-three years later), threw a lighted German phosphorous bomb out of the trench in which it had just landed, an action for which he was awarded the Military Cross. Wilson was a chemical engineer from Ipswich and later made a number of improvements to the equipment the Specials were using, especially by reducing gas leakages and by developing a method of getting a number of cylinders to discharge simultaneously.

Over the succeeding months, there were other improvements in technology. The cumbersome, leaky iron connecting pipes were replaced with rubber hoses. The design of the gas masks was improved, removable goggles replacing a celluloid window. Cylinders were supplemented with projectors, which lobbed gas shells a quarter of a mile or so in the direction of the enemy. A projector was a steel tube eight inches in diameter and either two feet nine inches or four feet long. Mounted on a steel baseplate, it fired a gas-filled cylindrical drum at an angle of 45 degrees. Each projector weighed 120 pounds, the baseplate 40 pounds and the drum 'shell' 65 pounds. All had to be carried into position by hand. Grouped closely together, several hundred projectors could be fired simultaneously, but it was difficult to prepare a gas barrage of this kind without being seen and coming under enemy artillery fire.

The winter of 1915 in Flanders arrived early and was desperately wet and cold. Writing in *Margin Released*, J B Priestley rated the conditions of existence in the front line at the time as worse than German artillery bombardments, describing how he slithered along the muddy, water-filled trenches for day after day, heavily laden with coils of barbed wire, without hot food and sleepless.

Against the backcloth of continuing trench warfare and gas attacks in appalling conditions, five days home leave in February 1916 must have come as a wonderful, if brief, interlude for G.O.M. It was the first time that he was able to visit his mother in Bradford since he had marched off to France with his infantry regiment nearly ten months before. Returning to France, G.O.M. found that the Special Brigade had been reorganized. He was now in 'M' Company. It was to this 'band of brothers' that my godfather and all the honorary uncles of my childhood belonged. Three months later, G.O.M. was joined in the Special Brigade by his younger brother Rupert, a battle-hardened

infantry veteran at 18 years of age. G.O.M. had been very sad at having to leave Rupert behind when he transferred from the West Yorkshires and the two brothers must have been delighted to be back together again.

On 3 June 1916, the whole Special Brigade was reviewed on the common at its Helfaut base by the British Commander-in-Chief, Sir Douglas Haig. Shortly afterwards, a number of the gas companies in the Special Brigade were moved to the Somme in preparation for Haig's massive – and disastrous – British assault on 1 July. G.O.M.'s 'M' Company was not among them, but continued fighting, taking part in diversionary gas attacks just north of Armentières. G.O.M.'s laconic note of a night gas attack at Plug Street (Ploegsteert) on 30 June, the day before the Somme offensive was launched, is 'Slightly wounded. Arm & Jaw.' I don't remember seeing any trace of these particular wounds on my father, but I do recall the permanent scars of shrapnel wounds on his fingers, visible to the day he died.

These minor wounds were perhaps a small price that G.O.M. paid for not being involved in the Battle of the Somme. This has registered in popular memory as the archetypal conflict on the Western Front – and with good reason. On 1 July 1916, the first day of the allied assault, there were more than 57,000 British casualties, of whom over 19,000 were killed. 60 per cent of the casualties were caused by German machine-gun fire. Some regiments were virtually wiped out. The 11th Battalion of the East Lancashire Regiment, recruited from the small Lancashire town of Accrington and known as the 'Accrington Pals', lost 234 killed and 360 wounded. By nightfall, there were just 135 survivors. The 10th Battalion of the West Yorkshire Regiment suffered 710 casualties. The battle rolled on inconclusively until November 1916, when both the allied and German armies were exhausted. Over the four months, allied casualties totalled some 600,000, of whom two-thirds were British. German casualties were similar.

G.O.M.'s involvements in gas attacks in various Western Front sectors continued throughout 1916. Neuve Chapelle and again Neuve Chapelle: Hill 70 and again Hill 70: Plug Street, Plug Street and again Plug Street. The familiar place names recur in his notes (he had not kept a detailed diary after the traumatic events of the first day of the Battle of Loos) time after time, witness to the static character of the war on the Western Front. Only the infantry formations to which he was attached change as, weakened by heavy casualties, they were rotated in the front line – 41st Division, 23rd Division, 7th Division,

25th Division ... In September, G.O.M. was promoted from
Corporal to Sergeant. Looking back in later years, he always thought
of himself as 'Sergeant Mitchell', even though he was eventually
commissioned as a Second Lieutenant.

G.O.M.'s notes for the bitter winter of 1917 continue in a similar
vein, each brief entry of date and place indicating another gas attack,
with all the manhandling of cylinders or projectors and the syn-
chronised launching of gas. If the wind was favourable, most of it
drifted towards the enemy, with only a residue leaving G.O.M. and
his companions coughing and spluttering in the front line discharge
emplacements. Of course, if the wind changed direction, they had to
hope that their primitive gas masks would keep most of the gas from
reaching their lungs. To make matters worse, many of the attacks
were at night – 11 pm occurs several times in the notes as the hour at
which a gas attack took place, even 2.30 and 3 am. Frequently, as
soon as the gas Specials appeared in the front trench to prepare a gas
attack, the infantry moved back to the reserve trench to avoid
accidental or leaky discharges. This left G.O.M. and his mates feeling
very exposed in the event of a surprise German attack.

One particular small scale assault proved to be a disaster for
G.O.M. and his 'M' Company comrades. G.O.M.'s note for 1 March
1917 laconically records 'Gas attack (4th Canadian Div) Vimy Ridge.
3 am' but the detail is spelled out by Donald Richter in *Chemical
Soldiers*:

> In the early hours of 1 March, ['M' Company] released the first wave
> of 1,308 cylinders of White Star (the usual 50 per cent chlorine and 50
> per cent phosgene mixture) in an almost ideal west-southwest wind of
> eight to ten mph. Enemy shellfire, however, punctured several pipes
> during the discharge, filling the trenches with gas. Casualties in 'M'
> Company totalled nine killed and thirty gassed and wounded, the great
> majority of gas casualties caused either by shattered pipes or careless-
> ness in removing helmets too soon.

A change in the wind forced the cancellation of the discharge of the
second wave of cylinders and when the Canadian infantry went over
the top they '... encountered a lethal combination of withering
machine-gun fire and lingering gas.' They sustained heavy casualties
and the failed raid was the subject of mutual recrimination between
the Canadian officers and the Special Brigade. Meanwhile, G.O.M.
was burying some of his 'M' Company comrades and helping others
back to the casualty clearing station.

On 7 July, the gas Special Brigade's base at Helfaut was visited by King George V and the heir to the throne, the Prince of Wales, though, unlike other such visits to the front, this received no publicity at the time.[2] Indeed, it is not mentioned in G.O.M.'s notes.

Later that month, after a long interval of sixteen months, G.O.M. left France for another spell of home leave, this time ten days. By contrast with the royal visit, it is spelled out in capital letters in G.O.M.'s notes. One particular day stands out – 28 July, uniquely underlined twice:

28.7.17 Joey

Joey was the name he always used for Josephine Garner, whom he married just over a year later. I am convinced that this note records the date when he proposed marriage to his future wife, my mother, and was accepted. Two days later, he said goodbye to his 19-year-old fiancée and returned to the front line. This was just one of many millions of such partings during the First World War – sons, husbands, fiancés, boyfriends being seen off to the war, all across Europe and beyond. In ten million cases, it was a final parting: the man never came back. My mother and father – and their children, grandchildren and future generations – were among the fortunate ones.

Back at the front, the increasingly familiar pattern of the gas attack began to establish itself. Hauling the cylinders up through winding, debris-filled communication trenches into their allotted positions, each 120 pound cylinder slung on poles between two men, with a third as relief for long carries; the opening up of the deafening artillery barrage on the enemy trenches; our guns falling silent preparatory to the infantry going 'over the top' through the cloud of gas and smoke; the tat-tat-tat of machine-gun fire, theirs and ours; the German artillery's counter-barrage just as G.O.M. and the other lads of the Special Brigade were trying to disconnect their cylinders or get

---

[2]There is a fascinating Appendix in Donald Richter's *Chemical Soldiers* about the aftermath of this visit. In the early 1930s, when Foulkes (who had been promoted to brigadier-general in 1917) was preparing the manuscript of his book *Gas! The Story of the Special Brigade* for publication, Buckingham Palace refused him permission to publish any photographs of the royal family that associated them with gas warfare, including their attendance at gas demonstrations. The outcome was that Foulkes had to leave out all pictures of the royal family except one of King George V crossing a bridge over a trench, captioned 'His Majesty at the Front (attended by the Author).' In fact, the photo was taken during the royal visit to the Helfaut base. However, permission has been granted by the Imperial War Museum to include in this book a photograph of King George V and the Prince of Wales (later king Edward VIII) visiting the Special Brigade's Helfaut base on 7 July 1917 (see illus. 15).

their projectors back from the front line; the sense of relief when they were out of range of the torrent of shells; brewing up tea using a candle stub in a bully beef tin; mordant exchanges of news about who had been hit or gassed and who had had a near squeak; a joke or some horseplay to relieve the tension while waiting for news of what had happened to the infantry – all too often back in reduced numbers in their own trenches without ever having reached the German front line.

In October 1917, G.O.M. found himself wearing a Belgian infantry helmet. 'M' Company had been temporarily attached to the 2nd Belgian Division, which was holding part of the line in one of those 'live and let live' sectors, where there was a tacit understanding between the two sides that no serious offensive action would be undertaken. The Allied High Command had decided to bring this to an end with a surprise gas attack. To conceal the presence of British soldiers, G.O.M. and his 'M' Company comrades wore Belgian helmets while they brought up all equipment needed for launching gas. When the gas was launched on 9 October, followed by an assault by Belgian infantry, the Germans were taken completely by surprise. A modest tactical victory was achieved – with a considerable boost to the morale of the Belgian army.

At the end of 1917, G.O.M. had another spell of home leave, this time a whole month over Christmas, spent in Bradford with his mother, fiancée and friends. It was his first Christmas at home for four years and it must have been difficult for him in mid-January to put his uniform back on and return to the front line. Two months later, in March, he spent two weeks in a military hospital in France. There is no indication in his notes of the reason for this. I don't think it was because he was wounded. At first, I thought he might have been a victim of the Spanish 'flu epidemic which raged throughout Europe and beyond for two years, but the date is a few months too early. Measles and mumps were rife in the Special Brigade at the time, so perhaps it was one of these.

In any event, the spell in hospital proved to be yet another stroke of luck for G.O.M. Early in 1918, there had been growing apprehension in the British and French commands that a major assault was being prepared by the Germans. In the east, the revolutions of February and October 1917 had led to Russia's exit from the war. The Germans rapidly transferred huge numbers of men and guns from the Eastern to the Western front. By the middle of March 1918, there were no fewer than 162 German divisions in the west, thirty more than the combined French and British total.

10. *British infantry leaving their front line trench to advance to the attack through a cloud of gas and smoke, Battle of Loos 25 September 1915 (IWM HU 63277B)*

11. *Bursting gas shells, Cambrin 13 October 1915 – an apparently empty landscape, but there are thousands of British and German soldiers below ground level in dugouts and trenches, marked by white stripes of chalk (IWM Q29004)*

12 Returning walking wounded, Cambrin 13 October 1915 (IWM Q29005)

13. British troops blinded by gas wait outside an Advance Dressing Station, near Béthune (IWM Q11586)

14. *Sgt Martin 'Syd' Fox with gas cylinders, 1916 (REM 6911-03)*

15. *King George V and the Prince of Wales – later King Edward VIII and Duke of Windsor – at Helfaut gas base, 7 July 1917 (IWM Q5610)*

16. *G.O.M as Sergeant RE Special Brigade*

17. Josephine Garner

18. The marriage of G.O.M. and Josephine Garner, 25 September 1918

19 *G. O. M. in later life as Chief Colourist ICI Dyestuffs Division*

On 21 March, General Ludendorff launched Operation Michael, a massive assault which rolled back the allied defences (see map 2). Following a five-hour artillery bombardment across a fifty-mile front, seventy-six German divisions attacked the British line, held by just twenty-eight divisions. On the first day, 7,000 British soldiers had been killed and 21,000 taken prisoner. In the days that followed, every available British soldier was involved in trying to slow the German advance and bring the disorganised retreat to a halt. In the first fortnight of April, six companies of the Special Brigade had had their revolvers replaced by rifles so that they could fight alongside the infantry in trying to stem the German attack, especially in front of Amiens, where the Germans had advanced up to a depth of forty miles and had almost reached the suburbs.

By the time G.O.M. returned to the front line from hospital, counterattacks were being mounted. Instead of being deployed with the infantry, 'M' Company was engaged in three gas projector attacks on German positions at Hill 70 – familiar territory – near Loos. The situation continued to be serious, with Ludendorff launching a second offensive, Operation Georgette, on 9 April. Again, many of the other gas companies were involved in infantry warfare and suffered heavy casualties. By 29 April the German advance on this sector of the front had run its course and in May Ludendorff diverted his last remaining reserves further south for a series of convulsive assaults on Paris. However, the exhausted French and British armies defending the French capital were bolstered by fresh United States troops, at long last beginning to arrive in significant numbers. The final German assault in July got to within fifty-six miles of Paris, which came under shelling from long-range guns, including the notorious 'Big Bertha'.

Around this time, G.O.M.'s company commander, Capt D M Wilson, was seconded to help the rapidly growing United States forces in France with gas training. Six American gas companies trained with the Special Brigade and G.O.M.'s 'M' Company was strengthened by the addition of a US platoon. Wilson's place was taken by Capt Lewis Casson. Casson was already an established actor and director on the London stage, notably of plays by Shakespeare and George Bernard Shaw. He had been transferred to the Special Brigade when the army discovered that back in the previous century he had, without completing it, started a degree course in chemistry. According to his son, John Casson, in *Lewis and Sybil* (1972):

One night [Lewis Casson] had been ordered to lay a large number of cylinders of phosgene out in No Man's Land. There was himself, a sergeant and a dozen privates from the REs and he was to have a large carrying party of a hundred Australians. The Australians, for some reason, failed to turn up and so Lewis took his baker's dozen engineers and they did the job on their own. Lewis got a Military Cross for the night's work, and a wound in his shoulder from a piece of shrapnel.[3]

In August 1918 the tide began to turn, with the allied forces rolling back the heavily depleted and demoralised German divisions. By September, British, French and newly arrived American troops were reoccupying the ground that had been lost a few months earlier. For the first time in four years, an advance by allied troops was actually accelerating rather than grinding to a halt.

It was at that this time that G.O.M.'s active participation in the fighting ceased. He returned to the Special Brigade base at Helfaut on 1 September, after taking part in two projector attacks with the 4th Division, and his notes come to an end on 20 September with the single word in capitals – **ENGLAND.**

---

[3]After the war, Lewis Casson went on to become one of the leading figures in British drama, forming a notable theatrical duo with his wife, Sybil Thorndike, and was knighted in 1945. When Casson was performing at the Opera House in Manchester in July 1959, he had an exchange of letters with G.O.M. in which he referred to the incident when he won the MC, saying that he had '. . . a hell of a row with the Special Brigade staff brass hats', as they had backed up the Aussies.

CHAPTER 8

Peace – Well, for a While

WITHIN A WEEK OF GETTING BACK from the front, G.O.M. was married to his beloved Joey, Josephine Garner, at St Marie's Catholic Church, in Halifax, Yorkshire. A clutch of wedding photographs that survive show a tall G.O.M. in a Royal Engineers sergeant's uniform, with his shoulder height bride (see illus. 18). There was also a photograph of the couple in the local evening paper, the *Halifax Courier*, under the heading 'A Military Wedding'. As was the custom then, the bride's appearance was described in detail – 'very tastefully attired in ivory satin. She wore a veil of Brussels lace over a cap of old French pearl lace and carried a sheaf of lilies. Her single ornament was a gold chain with pearl pendant, the gift of the mother of the bridegroom.' The newspaper report states that the bride was 'attended' by her niece, Margaret,[1] who wore '. . . a Kate Greenaway gown of ivory silk, and a wreath of white velvet laurel leaves.' The two bridesmaids had '. . . dainty gowns of blue silk in two shades and wore pearl brooches, gifts of the bridegroom.' To G.O.M., it must have all seemed like a dream by contrast with the blood, mud and filth of Flanders, only a week or so behind him.

G.O.M.'s best man was one of his Special Brigade comrades, the recently promoted Lt Clements. Though he later played quite a large part in family life and lore, I never knew his first name – he was always 'Uncle Clem'. G.O.M.'s younger brother, Rupert, does not appear in the photographs: perhaps he had been unable to get leave from the front.

It is only recently that I have realized the significance of the date of the wedding – 25 September, exactly three years after the date of the Battle of Loos. No doubt chance played a big part in G.O.M. being granted marital leave at this time, but for him this anniversary must have signified the triumph of hope over despair, of a peaceful future over a nightmare past.

---

[1]Margaret Sladdin, daughter of my mother's elder sister, Claire, was my cousin and was eight years old at the time of my parents' wedding. She lost her sight as she grew older but nevertheless brought up single-handed her three great-nieces, to whom she was always Aunty Margaret. She died in April 2003, at the age of 92.

G.O.M. and Josephine both came from Bradford, but were married ten miles away in Halifax, because this was the home of another of Josephine's older sisters, May, already married to Irvine Hodgson. May and Irvine, who was a dentist, lived at 212 Queens Road, Halifax, and it was from this house that Josephine made the short journey down Gibbet Street to St Marie's, to be 'given away' by her brother-in-law.

The liaison was, in Catholic terminology, a 'mixed marriage' – Josephine was a Catholic, while G.O.M. was Church of England. At that time, the Catholic Church had strict rules about mixed marriages. For example, the non-Catholic partner had to undertake that any children of the marriage would be brought up as Catholics (as my sister Joy and I were). Also, he or she, while not required to convert to Catholicism, had to undergo a short course of instruction by a Catholic priest in the rudiments of Catholic faith and practice.

Who was the priest who instructed G.O.M. in the hectic five days between his return from France and the date of his marriage? During my childhood, my parents frequently talked about Father John O'Connor, parish priest for thirty-two years of St Cuthbert's Catholic Church in Bradford. He was the model for 'Father Brown' in the detective stories of that name by G K Chesterton. Thea Cheshire, the daughter of my cousin Desmond Hodgson, tells me that G.O.M.'s Bradford home was in St Cuthbert's parish, so it is highly likely that it was Father John O'Connor[2] who instructed G.O.M. about Catholicism.

After the wedding, G.O.M. and Josephine, in her going-away outfit of '. . . stone cloth with white fox furs and hat to match' left for Harrogate, to spend the first part of their honeymoon at the Prospect Hotel. The second part was spent at the Marble Arch Hotel in London. A theatre programme has survived from that holiday – *Chu Chin Chow* at His Majesty's Theatre in the Haymarket, a long-running musical then in its third year. Though the honeymoon couple were far away from the Western front, the programme contained a grim reminder that this was a global war.

Arrangements have been made for warning of a threatened Air Raid to be communicated by the Military Authorities to this Theatre. On

---

[2]As well as being a friend of G K Chesterton, Father John O'Connor (1871–1952) was also a confidant of the great artist-craftsman Eric Gill, whom he commissioned to carve a set of Stations of the Cross for St Cuthbert's. In 1937, he was appointed Privy Chamberlain to Pope Pius XI, an office that carried the title of Monsignor.

receipt of any such warning the audience will be informed with a view to enable persons who may wish to proceed home, or to secure better shelter, to do so. Also to give any Naval and Military officers, whose duty requires them to go to their posts, the opportunity of immediately leaving the Theatre for this purpose.

The scale of bombing of London from the air in the First World War was, of course, nothing like the blitzes of World War Two, but 800 Londoners had been killed and 1,500 injured in air raids by Zeppelin airships and Gotha bombers in 1917 and 1918.

At the end of the honeymoon, Josephine saw her new husband off, not this time to the battlefields of France and Belgium, but to the tranquility of Cambridge, where he joined an Officer Cadet Battalion based at Pembroke College. It was while he was training to become a commissioned officer that the armistice bringing war to an end was declared on 11 November 1918. Among my most treasured possessions is a postcard sent to him from Bradford on that day from his mother and his bride, with the simple message 'Peace-day'.

G.O.M. completed his officer training course at Cambridge and received his Commission as Temporary Second Lieutenant on 14 May 1919, being demobilised shortly afterwards without returning to active service. The Commission was back in his old infantry regiment, the West Yorkshires, though when he was placed on the regular army reserve of officers three years later, on 19 May 1922, it was in the Royal Engineers.

* * *

G.O.M. had been one of the lucky ones. If the German shell that had crashed through the roof of his billet at Croix Blanche had been live rather than a dud; if just one of a thousand or more bullets that zinged by him had been a foot to the left or right, or up or down; if . . . if . . . he would have joined the ten million others whose lives came to an abrupt and early end in the First World War. He survived, with some minor wounds and a respiratory system permanently blighted by many lungfuls of poison gas. He went on to enjoy a rewarding professional life as a dyestuffs chemist and a blissfully happy marriage to his beloved Joey, who gave birth to a daughter, Joy, and to me. Twenty years on from the 1918 Armistice, though, I can remember the deep depression that came over the family at the time when Britain and France capitulated to Hitler at Munich − and the despair a year later in 1939 when Germany invaded Poland, precipitating the Second World War. For G.O.M., it was as if he and his comrades, the survivors and the dead, had fought in vain.

Indeed, the decade that followed 1939 saw all four members of our family in uniform of one kind or another. On the eve of the Second World War, my mother wore the green uniform of the WVS (Women's Voluntary Service – now Women's Royal Voluntary Service) as she helped organise the evacuation of children from Manchester in anticipation of air attacks by the Luftwaffe. My sister Joy was next. She joined the WAAF (Women's Auxiliary Air Force) and was stationed at Tangmere, a front line fighter aerodrome in Sussex during the 1940 Battle of Britain. After the fall of France, G.O.M. joined the Home Guard ('Dad's Army') at his place of work, ICI Dyestuffs Division in Blackley, north Manchester. On 12 August 1940, nearly twenty-five years after the Battle of Loos, and when the Battle of Britain was entering its climactic phase, he wrote to Joy at Tangmere:

Largely due to my inherent laziness and despite sundry twinges of conscience I have withheld my valuable services in the present crisis. However it has been decided to form an LDV [Local Defence Volunteers, later Home Guard] unit at the works, so I have joined up. When on duty ICI [Imperial Chemical Industries] provide supper and breakfast! No grubbing about in some broken down hut for your old man. Do your fighting in comfort is my motto. We had our first parade tonight and it reminded me of the 'Dook's' [Duke of Wellington] saying about his troops: 'I don't know what they do to the enemy, but by God they frighten me'! The ex-servicemen were fallen in under an ex-RSM [Regimental Sergeant Major] and after sundry creakings we limbered up and gave a demonstration of squad drill at a respectable light infantry step (about 130 paces to the minute). Anyway, I suppose it will turn up all right in the end, but Heaven help us when we get our guns!

I was the last of the four of us to go into uniform, just over two years after the Second World War ended. My National Service saw me conscripted as a private into the Northumberland Fusiliers before being commissioned as a 2nd Lt in the Royal Artillery. Compared with G.O.M., I was the lucky one. In two years in the army, I never heard a shot fired in anger. Now I am the lone survivor from that south Manchester suburban family and have lived to see my country being branded an international aggressor, led by politicians who have no sense of history, no understanding of the loss and suffering that war brings to its victims, no realisation that the primary duty of a statesman is to explore every opportunity of finding a peaceful

solution to international problems rather then deploying bombs and bullets. Along with millions of my fellow countrymen and women, I feel ashamed that the growing counts of Iraqi and Afghani dead are relegated to a minor place in the daily news bulletins, if they are reported at all.

*   *   *

My father was not a professional soldier. He had joined the local territorial army battalion in Bradford as a part-time 'Saturday night soldier' in 1911 and had responded immediately to the call to arms on the day that war broke out on 4 August 1914. He had seen service in the front line throughout the conflict, notably on the first day of the Battle of Loos, but also in many other engagements, large and small. Without doubt, the war – even though he once said it was '90 per cent boredom' – was the central, most significant experience of his whole life, as it must have been to any young man of whatever nationality who went through a similar ordeal.

Yet, though he treasured the medals he had been awarded, G.O.M. did not talk much about the war. When he did, it was to emphasise the humour, the comradeship, rather than the horrors of life in the trenches. He was not a flag-waving, jingoistic, self-proclaimed patriot. I can remember asking him once what he felt about the war. His reply seemed to me rather prosaic at the time – 'it was a job that had to be done'. In retrospect, though, this was probably an approach he shared with many of his contemporaries, not least his fellow-Bradfordian and near neighbour, J B Priestley, who adopts a similar stance in his autobiographical *Margin Released*.

At the other end of the political spectrum from Priestley, the Conservative Prime Minister Harold Macmillan had a very similar view. Looking back on what had happened more than forty years beforehand, he wrote in *Winds of Change*, that:

> War is a terrible disaster for a nation, even the old wars of pre-nuclear days. They reveal dark forces and bring into play brutal passions; and, as we have now learnt, victory brings almost as many dangers as defeat. This is no doubt true of whole peoples. But it cannot be denied that to the individual war may and does bring an extraordinary thrill – a sense of comradeship – a sense of teamship and a sense of triumph. Everything that the King said so nobly to his men before Agincourt was as true in 1914 as it had been in 1415. Any man who, of his own choice, misses or shirks such an opportunity is not a complete man. I have always felt a certain contempt for those 'gentlemen in England now abed', whether in the First War or the Second, who voluntarily

missed their chance or chose to avoid danger by seeking positions of security.[3]

Macmillan makes clear, though, how the appalling waste of lives determined a change in the character of the war as the four years dragged by:

> The long-drawn out battles of the autumn of 1917 oppressed me with their futility. I had at least enough knowledge to read between the lines of official statements. I and many others felt bitterly over all this; perhaps more bitterly, because we were at home, than had we been in the field – or rather, in the mud.

There was no military tradition in our family. My father was, so far as I know, the first ever to wear uniform, serving from the first day that war broke out through to the Armistice and beyond. He never boasted about his exploits. He said little about the hardship and suffering he had endured for more than four years or his anguish at seeing comrades blown to bits, maimed or gassed. It was a job that had to be done and he had played his part. I am proud to be his son.

---

[3]This attitude helps to explain the continuing contempt in which Macmillan held R A Butler, his Conservative Party contemporary, though Butler was too young to fight in the First World War. Macmillan was determined that he should never be leader of the Conservative Party – and he succeeded in his objective.

Afterword

THE CORE OF THIS BOOK is the trench diary kept by my father, G.O.M. (George Oswald Mitchell), from the day the 1/6th Battalion West Yorkshire Regiment left for France on 15 April 1915 to 25 September 1915, the end of first day of the Battle of Loos. Manuscript notes in his printed copy of Standing Orders and Regulations supplement this source. These refer to G.O.M.'s movements and the various gas attacks he was involved with during the rest of the war. Both the diary and the Standing Orders and Regulations are lodged in the Imperial War Museum Department of Documents in London. A copy of the diary is also held in the Royal Engineers Library at Chatham, Kent. Selected extracts from the diary have previously been quoted in Philip Warner, *The Battle of Loos* (1976, republished 2000), Donald Richter, *Chemical Soldiers* (1994), Judith Cook, *Priestley* (1997) and Niall Cherry, *Most Unfavourable Ground – The Battle of Loos 1915* (2005).

I have also drawn on much detailed information in *History of the 6th Battalion West Yorkshire Regiment – Volume I – 1/6th Battalion*. This was published in 1921, shortly after the end of the First World War, and was written by the Battalion historian, Captain E V Tempest. Captain Tempest served with the Battalion during the war, was awarded the DSO and MC for gallantry in action and was wounded on 11 October 1917. He certainly knew what he was writing about. There is also valuable information about the 1/6th Battalion in a book by the Regimental historian, Laurie Magnus, *The West Riding Territorials in the Great War*. While the author did not himself serve with the unit, this account has the virtue of immediacy, as it was published in 1920.

The work of the gas Special Companies and Brigade of the Royal Engineers, in which G.O.M. served from the time it was set up in 1915, is dealt with in C H Foulkes, *'Gas!' The Story of the Special Brigade* (1934). Foulkes set up and commanded the Special Brigade so, while it is an indispensable record, the author's stress on the importance of the part that gas warfare played in securing victory needs to be taken with a sniff of scepticism. Donald Richter,

Chemical Soldiers (1994) is an outstanding account of the British use of gas, drawing on a wide variety of sources, including personal reminiscences as well as official papers. These include the *Special Brigade Newsletters*. Fifty issues were published between 1958 and 1981, printing the reminiscences and opinions of those who survived. A set of these is lodged in the library of the Royal Engineers: I have been privileged to be allowed access to them. Edward M Spiers makes a useful input to the debate about the importance (or otherwise) of gas in 'Chemical Warfare in the First World War', a contribution to the British Commission for Military History's seminar commemorating the 80th anniversary of the Battle of the Somme, *Look to Your Front* (1999). Ludwig Haber, *The Poisonous Cloud* (1986) is a magisterial account of the development and use of gas as a weapon: it gains in authority from the fact that the author is the son of Fritz Haber, the German chemist who pioneered the use of gas in warfare. Simon Jones, *World War I Gas Warfare Tactics and Equipment* (2007) reviews offensive and defensive gas equipment and how it was deployed. Paul Voivenel and Paul Martin, *La Guerre des gaz 1915–1918* (1919, republished 2004) is a near-contemporary account of the effects of gas on its victims written by two French doctors who were attached to the specialist 'ambulance Z', which dealt with the French army's gas casualties.

G.O.M. was in the front line on the first day of the Battle of Loos on 25 September 1915. As mentioned above, extracts from his diary are quoted in Philip Warner, *The Battle of Loos* (1976, republished 2000) along with material that the author received in reply to a letter he wrote in the *Daily Telegraph* asking for survivors of the battle, or their relatives, to let him see diaries or reminiscences. This specialist work contains personal accounts not found elsewhere, but has been criticised for a number of inaccuracies. G.O.M.'s diary is also cited briefly in Niall Cherry, *Most Unfavourable Ground – The Battle of Loos 1915* (2005). This is a comprehensive, thorough and lucid account that is unlikely to be superseded for many years, if ever. The new era of Internet publication has seen a description of the battle published (apparently anonymously) under *The Long, Long Trail* title by Milverton Associates Ltd (www.1914-1918.net/Battles). There is an account of the fighting at Loos in Robert Graves, *Goodbye to All That* (1929, revised 1957). At the time, Graves was a 2nd Lt in the 2nd Bn Royal Welch Fusiliers. The book has made a tremendous impact over the decades as an anti-war tract. However, Paul Fussell, the outstanding critic of the literature of the First World War, issues

a caution that it should be read as fiction disguised as autobiography rather than as a factual account of what happened. A surprisingly neglected account of the second wave of the Battle of Loos appears in *The Winds of Change* (1966) by the former Prime Minister, Harold Macmillan, who was a subaltern in the Grenadier Guards at the time.

More generally, there seems to be no end to the flow of books about the First World War. It seems as though we are still trying to find an explanation for four years of conflict that claimed so many young lives. In retrospect, it appears to have been as much an encounter between flesh and steel, in which there could only ever be one winner, as a struggle for victory between nations. There was no ideological basis for the war, which swept up most of the so-called 'civilised' countries of the world into its maelstrom. Heated debates continue about the causes and conduct of the conflict and extend well beyond the world of academic historians. Reviewing the whole literature is an impossible task. All I can do is pick out those books I have found particularly stimulating.

On the origins of the war, Paul Kennedy, *The Rise and Fall of the Great Powers* (1988) analyses the interplay of economic change and military conflict over the five-hundred-year period 1500–2000. It includes a detailed and perceptive analysis of the political and economic rivalry between Britain and Germany from 1885 to the outbreak of war in 1914. Keith Wilson's edited collection of conference papers *Decisions for War, 1914* (1995) is valuable in tracking the path to war taken by some of the lesser combatants, such as Serbia, Belgium, Japan and the Ottoman Empire as well as the more powerful nations. H W Koch, *The Origins of the First World War* (1972, republished 1984) is another edited collection of contributions, in this case all by German historians, dealing with the controversial questions surrounding Germany's war aims.

Three comprehensive studies of the 1914-18 conflict, all titled *The First World War*, are by Martin Gilbert (1994), John Keegan (1998) and Hew Strachan (2003). The latter is unusual in paying attention to theatres of war away from France and Flanders, such as Italy, the Balkans, the Middle East and Africa, and for reproducing a number of colour photographs. These give the lie to the received impression that, while the Second World War was fought in colour, the First World War was fought in black and white. Arthur Banks, *A Military Atlas of the First World War* (1975) offers much more than the word 'atlas' might suggest. Lyn Macdonald's series of books about the Western Front, *1914: The Dawn of Hope* (1987), *1915: The Death*

of Innocence (1993), *Somme* (1983), *They Called It Passchendaele* (1978) and *To the Last Man: Spring 1918* (1998) are a successful synthesis of politics, military strategy and the experience of the ordinary soldier in the trenches. Richard Holmes, *The Western Front* (1999) is a good short account of the war in the trenches. Denis Winter, *Death's Men: Soldiers of the Great War* (1978) remains an outstanding trench-eye view of war in north-eastern France and Flanders.

In recent years there has been a welcome increase in the number of books drawing on the diaries and letters of ordinary soldiers. These include Malcom Brown, *Tommy Goes to War* (1978, republished 2005) and *1918: Year of Victory* (1998), Richard Holmes, *Tommy* (2004) and Ilana R Bet-El *Conscripts* (1999). Max Arthur, *Forgotten Voices of the Great War* (2002) draws on a collection of taped interviews held by the Imperial War Museum. Lord Reith's *Wearing Spurs* (1966) is a Glaswegian Son of the Manse's lively and engaging account of life as a young Territorial subaltern. In the spring and early summer of 1915 the future Director General of the BBC fought in the same sector of the Western Front as G.O.M. Michael Senior, *No Finer Courage* (2004) is an excellent portrayal of how a Buckinghamshire village was affected by the war, including a detailed account of what happened to the young men who went to fight in France.

It may be that the First and Second World Wars will be the twin summits of our understanding of the soldier's experience of war, because of the huge volume of written, first-hand accounts available to historians. For example, the United States and British soldiers involved in the invasion and occupation of Afghanistan and Iraq seem understandably to rely more on ephemeral emails and mobile phone calls than manuscript accounts of what they have lived through. What raw material will survive for future historians and readers?

The impact of war on civilians in the Second World War has received a good deal of attention, with life in Britain between 1914 and 1918 being comparatively neglected. An exception is Steve Humphries and Richard van Emden, *All Quiet on the Home Front* (2003), which draws on newspapers and government reports as well as on letters and diaries. The experiences and perspectives of German civilians and soldiers are covered comprehensively in Laurence V Moyer, *Victory Must Be Ours: Germany in the Great War 1914–1918* (1995).

On a larger canvas, Niall Ferguson in *The War of the World* (2006) tackles the extraordinary violence of the twentieth century – 'His-

tory's Age of Hatred' – in which the First World War played a seminal role. The same author's *The Pity of War* (1998) challenges many widely held received opinions about the First World War and deals chillingly but convincingly with such issues as the relationship between the number of casualties and expenditure on armaments – the killing power of the pound sterling, franc, rouble and deutschmark.

The course of the international negotiations that led to the 1919 Treaty of Versailles, together with the implications of the Treaty's provisions for the future of Europe, are the subject of Richard M Watt, *The Kings Depart* (1969) and Margaret Macmillan, *Paris 1919* (2001). It is not difficult to trace back many festering European problems of today – especially ethnic identity, nationhood and national boundaries in south-eastern Europe – to Versailles.

Fiction set in the First World War continues to be an expanding genre and deserves a critical review all on its own, which I am not equipped to undertake. The novels of Pat Barker's Regeneration trilogy – *Regeneration* (1991), *The Eye in the Door* (1993) and *The Ghost Road* (1995) – have brought the First World War to life for a new generation of readers, though I find the mixture of fact and fiction uneasy at times. Sebastian Faulks's *Birdsong* (1993) is a remarkably successful attempt to convey the thoughts and experiences of a front line soldier: it left me shattered. In *All Quiet on the Western Front* (1929), Erich Maria Remarque, who served in the German army from 1915 to the Armistice, wrote a novel that depicts a small group of soldiers gradually dwindling in number as the war grinds on – and finally vanishing. There are remarkable portrayals of the ordinary soldier's fear of gas. The year after publication, it was made into a notable film by Lewis Milestone. It remains one of the cornerstones of anti-war literature, as does the play by R C Sherriff, *Journey's End* (1928). C E Montague's *Disenchantment* (1922) is not fiction, but an extended essay on the folly and heroism of the Western Front, based on the author's experience in Flanders. Modris Eksteins, *Rites of Spring* (1989) is an illuminating analysis of the war's cultural context while Paul Fussell's *The Great War and Modern Memory* (1975) remains an absorbing guide to its prose and poetry.

APPENDIX A

Ranks and Formations

THE SYSTEM OF RANKS AND FORMATIONS in the British army remained largely unchanged for generations. The following notes summarise who did what at the time of the First World War, focusing on the infantry. However, they should not be interpreted too rigidly. In practice, there was considerable fluidity. This was especially true in the ebb and flow of battle, when soldiers with quite junior ranks might find themselves commanding large formations.

The basic rank was **Private** (abbreviated to Pte). The equivalent rank in the Royal Artillery was **Gunner** and in the Royal Engineers, **Sapper**. There were far more privates and equivalents than all the other ranks put together. For example, when G.O.M. sailed with 'C' Company of the 1/6th Battalion of the West Yorkshire Regiment for France on 15 April 1915, the company consisted of 197 privates, 52 non-commissioned officers (NCOs) and six commissioned officers.

The lowest ranking NCO was **Lance-Corporal** (L/Cpl), who wore a single chevron, familiarly known as a 'stripe', on his upper sleeve. Next was a full **Corporal** (Cpl), with two stripes. The equivalent Royal Artillery ranks were **Lance-Bombardier** and **Bombardier**. The ranks of the **Sergeants** (Sgt) had their own complex hierarchy, with the more senior known as Warrant Officers. In ascending order of seniority above the plain three-stripers were **Company Sergeant-Major** (CSM) and **Regimental Sergeant-Major** (RSM). The latter, in spite of the word 'Regimental', was the most senior NCO in a battalion. There were also **Quarter-Master Sergeant**s (QMS) responsible for supplies. The RSM was by far the most powerful figure on the ordinary soldier's horizon, having a much greater influence on his daily life than the more remote commissioned officers. In the first volume of his autobiography, *Winds of Change*, Harold Macmillan quotes a former Grenadier Guards officer as saying, in 1914: 'When I joined, my battalion was run by the Sergeant-Major, and it was damned good. When I left, it was run by the Adjutant, and wasn't too bad. Now, they tell me, the Commanding Officer is trying to run this battalion. All I can say is, God help us!'

Among the commissioned officers, the most junior were the
Second-Lieutenant (2nd Lt or 2Lt), whose cuffs carried a single star
or 'pip', and the two-pip **Lieutenant** (Lt). As the war went on, pips
and other officers' insignia came to be worn on shoulder epaulettes
instead of cuffs. Younger generations, brought up on a diet of US war
films, should note that the English pronunciation *is Lef-tenant*, not
the American *Loo-tenant*. Second-Lieutenants and Lieutenants were
known as subalterns and were addressed orally as 'Mr' – for example,
after inspecting a platoon, the company commander might say 'Carry
on, Mr Whitaker', not 'Carry on, Lt Whitaker'.

Next up came **Captain** (Capt) with three pips.

Officers of Field Rank, in ascending order of seniority, were:

- **Major** (Maj) with a single crown as insignia;
- **Lieutenant-Colonel** (Lt Col) – one crown and one star;
- **Colonel** (Col) – one crown and two stars.

Above the Field Officers came the Generals. In ascending order, these
were:

- **Brigadier-General** (Brig Gen) – crossed swords and baton;
- **Major-General** (Maj Gen) – crossed swords and one star;
- **Lieutenant-General** (Lt Gen) – crossed swords, one crown;
- **General** (Gen) – crossed swords, one crown and one star.

In the early part of the war, there was a marked difference in
background and upbringing between commissioned officers on the
one hand and 'other ranks' – that is, NCOs and Privates – on the
other. Commissioned officers had in the main been to public (that is
independent, private) schools, while other ranks had been educated at
local authority schools. Of course, this divide was not absolutely rigid
and broke down progressively as the war continued, with many
commissioned officers being promoted from the ranks. My father,
G.O.M., was a case in point. Educated at a local authority grammar
school and technical college, he enlisted as a Private on the first day
that war broke out. He was subsequently promoted to Corporal, then
Sergeant. Finally, after formal training as an Officer Cadet, he
received the 'King's Commission' as a Second-Lieutenant.

*   *   *

In the infantry, the basic formation was a **Section**. Its size might vary
between eight and fifteen men and it was normally headed by a
Corporal. A **Platoon** consisted of four Sections and was headed by a
Lieutenant or Second-Lieutenant, with a Sergeant carrying out the

subaltern's orders. There was often a great deal of fluidity in the membership of sections and platoons. At full strength, a platoon numbered about sixty men, but numbers were often lower than this.

A **Company** (abbreviated to Coy), commanded by a Major or a Captain, consisted of four platoons, with a nominal strength of about 250. It was a more formal unit, usually known by a letter of the alphabet, and the one to which most soldiers gave their immediate allegiance. For example, when he was in the infantry, G.O.M. thought of himself as a member of 'C' Company of the 1/6th Battalion of the West Yorkshire Regiment. When he transferred to the Royal Engineers, he considered himself as belonging to 'M' Company of the Special Brigade. A **Battalion** (Bn), commanded by a Colonel or, more frequently, a Lieutenant-Colonel or Major, consisted of four companies, with a full strength of about 1,000, of whom about three-quarters might be engaged in any offensive operation. It would normally move, work and fight together as a single unit.

At this point, a digression is necessary to explain the concept of a **Regiment** (Regt). In the First World War, most infantry regiments were organised on a geographical (especially county) basis – Royal Berkshire Regiment, Devonshire Regiment, East Surrey Regiment, Argyll and Sutherland Highlanders, and so on. Within each regiment, there were numbered battalions. In the early days of the war, recruitment for different battalions was in different parts of the county. For example, G.O.M.'s 1/6th Battalion of the West Yorkshire Regiment was based in Bradford, while the 1/5th Battalion was drawn from York and the 1/7th and 1/8th Battalions from Leeds.

These were Territorial units, but the volunteers who joined up after the outbreak of war were sometimes grouped in what were known informally as 'Pals' battalions. This was especially true for recruits from northern industrial cities and towns. For example, the 16th and 18th Battalions of the West Yorkshire Regiment were the 1st and 2nd Bradford Pals, while the 15th Battalion were the Leeds Pals. However, the Battle of the Somme, which was launched on 1 July 1916, brought an end to this approach. A number of Pals' battalions – from Bradford, Leeds, Accrington and other towns in Yorkshire and Lancashire – were virtually wiped out on the first day. This caused a profound shock to civilian morale as clusters of neighbouring streets suddenly found that, in the course of a day or two, they had lost a whole generation of their young men. From then on, geographical distinctions in recruiting began to break down rapidly so that the supply of recruits was matched against demand as occasion arose: a

man from Gloucestershire might be allocated to the Northumberland Fusiliers and a Geordie from Tyneside to the Gloucesters.

The different battalions in a regiment did not necessarily fight alongside each other. In many cases, they were allocated to different brigades or divisions. For example, four battalions of the Middlesex Regiment were all involved in different divisions in the Battle of Loos, on different sectors of the battlefield. A Regiment was not normally, therefore, an operational unit on the battlefield. A notable exception to this was the formation in July 1915 of the Guards Division, comprising all twelve battalions of the Grenadier, Coldstream, Scots, Irish and Welsh Guards regiments.

A **Brigade** (Bde), led by a Brigadier-General, had four battalions up to the winter of 1917 – that is, about 4,000 men – and three afterwards. It was and continues to be a rather shadowy concept from the ordinary soldier's viewpoint. (An exception to this was the gas Special Brigade of the Royal Engineers, to which G.O.M. transferred from the infantry in 1915. This brigade was made up of companies rather than battalions and it was prominent in its members' loyalties, both at the time and in the post-war years.)

Each **Division** (Div) was commanded by a Major-General and would usually comprise three brigades, some 10,000–12,000 men in all. In the early stages of the war, there might also be as many as 5,000 horses. Royal Artillery gun batteries were normally attached to infantry at divisional level. While the composition of a division might change from time to time, a soldier would always know what division he was fighting with. As Denis Winter writes in *Death's Men*, a division:

> ... was the largest self-contained unit which moved about as a single unit. Bath-houses, cinemas, concerts and canteens all existed under the aegis of the division. Despite the size – a moving division occupied twenty miles of road and needed 188 lorry (and wagon) loads of equipment a day to keep it functioning – most men knew each other by sight.

To give an idea of the numbers involved in major battles, six divisions attacked on a three-mile front in the initial assault at the Battle of Loos, with a further three divisions in reserve. Probably well over 100,000 men in all were involved, including ancillary units.

An even larger formation was the **Corps**, commanded by a Lieutenant-General and consisting of three or four divisions. Its remoteness meant that it had little reality for the ordinary soldier. The

same is true of the **Army**, commanded by a General and consisting of three or four corps. By the end of the war, the British Expeditionary Force (BEF) in France and Flanders consisted of five armies.

The nominal strength of any unit or formation was rarely maintained once it had been in the front line and suffered casualties. After a major battle, as Lyn Macdonald writes in *1914* (1987), 'Brigades were reduced to the strength of battalions. Battalions were down to the strength of companies and companies at full muster were little more than platoons.' That was the grim reality of the war of attrition on the Western Front.

Old Comrades: 1/6th Battalion West Yorkshire Regiment

THIS FIRST LIST COMPRISES NCOs and men of 'C' Company of the 1/6th Battalion West Yorkshire Regiment who sailed with G.O.M. from Folkestone to Boulogne on SS *Victoria* on 15 April 1915 (commissioned officers are not listed), with ranks shown as on that date. They were G.O.M.'s comrades alongside whom he served in the infantry, before his transfer to the Royal Engineers in the summer of 1915.

Where a member of the company is known to have been killed in action or to have died on active service, this is indicated, together with his place of birth, if known, and army number. It will be seen that the great majority came from Yorkshire – and from the Bradford area particularly.

Gallantry medals are also shown: MC is the Military Cross, DCM the Distinguished Conduct Medal and MM the Military Medal. It is possible that the list of those killed is not comprehensive, as the 1/6th Battalion's records do not cover what happened to men after they were transferred to other units: a number may have been killed when with other regiments.

No information is listed about those who were wounded, taken prisoner of war or invalided out. The ratio of wounded to killed was about four to one. The list has been compiled mainly from information in Captain E V Tempest's *History of the 6th Battalion West Yorkshire Regiment Volume I – 1/6th Battalion* (1921). It is intended to be a remembrance of G.O.M.'s old comrades. It may also be of help to those who want to find out what happened to members of their family during the First World War.

CSM Barker, H – born Bradford, Yorks, no 240002: awarded MC and DCM: killed in action 25 April 1918
RQMS Welch, G
CQMS Packett, E A
Sgt Atwell, R
Sgt Buckley, E – born Bradford, Yorks, no 61: killed in action 21 December 1915

Sgt Derwent, R I
Sgt Jowett, H A
Sgt Martin, J R
Sgt Moorhouse, A – born Drighlington, Yorks, no 24007: killed in action 10 August 1918
Sgt Rendall, L P
Sgt Sandbach, F
Sgt Stevenson, H
Sgt Walmsley, W – born Bradford, Yorks, no 24001: awarded Croix de Guerre: died 27 October 1918
L/Sgt Cordingley, L
L/Sgt Hawkins, G W
Cpl Baxter, A C
Cpl Beldon, E
Cpl Ellis, W
Cpl Emmison, P C
Cpl Humphreys, G – no 2111: awarded DCM
Cpl Ingham, N – no 3005: killed in action 18 July 1916
Cpl Maddison, W
Cpl Sellars, S
Cpl Ward, W
L/Cpl Alvey, B
L/Cpl Beckett, J – born Bradford, Yorks, no 4937: killed in action 11 July 1916
L/Cpl Brown, J P
L/Cpl Capstick, W
L/Cpl Cockburn, F T
L/Cpl Dennis, W
L/Cpl Foster, R J – no 1799: awarded MM
L/Cpl Hale, T
L/Cpl Hindle, E
L/Cpl Howard, C
L/Cpl Humphries, W
L/Cpl Mitchell, H
L/Cpl Norton, H
L/Cpl Parker, W
L/Cpl Pollard, J
L/Cpl Speight, H
L/Cpl Sunter, T – no 2450: awarded DCM
L/Cpl Thompson, A
L/Cpl Thompson, J H
L/Cpl Underwood, S – born West Bowling, Yorks, no 240046: killed in action 25 April 1918

L/Cpl Wasteney, W – born Bradford, Yorks, no 1458: died of wounds 17 September 1916

L/Cpl White, J

Drummer Cates, H

Drummer Hawley, A

Drummer Kemp, D

Drummer Sprint, W

Pte Ackroyd, W

Pte Allum, C E

Pte Allum, W H – born Stanningley, Yorks, no 2426: killed in action 1 July 1916

Pte Arnold, N A

Pte Atkinson, J W

Pte Attenborough, J

Pte Balmforth, F

Pte Barker, S – born Bradford, Yorks, no 1483: killed in action 1 July 1916

Pte Benson, G L

Pte Bentley, C

Pte Best, A J

Pte Binks, W

Pte Binns, J

Pte Birkenshaw, J W

Pte Bloomer, A – born Eccleshill, Yorks, no 2070: killed in action 1 July 1916

Pte Bolton, G P

Pte Booth, H – born Bradford, Yorks, no 3048: killed in action 2 July 1916

Pte Bower, J E

Pte Boyes, A

Pte Bradley, E – no 3539: awarded DCM

Pte Bradley, T – born Bradford, Yorks, no 1756: awarded MM: killed in action 3 September 1916

Pte Bray, C

Pte Brocklehurst, F T

Pte Brooke, J W

Pte Brown, J – born Bradford, Yorks, no 241598: killed in action 25 April 1918

Pte Burke, T – no 3081: killed in action 15 December 1915

Pte Butterfield, A – no 241355: killed in action 26 April 1918

Pte Butterfield, T

Pte Carter, E C

Pte Carter, H W

Pte Cassarley, V – no 240344: awarded MM

Pte Chattaway, R

Pte Chippendale, S – no 240564: died 19 April 1917

Pte Clark, H C

Pte Clarke, F

Pte Clough, H – no 3396: killed in action 9 August 1915

Pte Cole, E

Pte Collins, N P

Pte Condor, G E W – no 2006: killed in action 11 October 1915

Pte Craven, C

Pte Craven, J

Pte Craven, T

Pte Crowther, P M

Pte Cryer, H – born Muswell Hill, London, no 1962: killed in action 19 August 1915

Pte Cure, G – born Manningham, Yorks, no 1543: killed in action 29 July 1915

Pte Cutcliffe, J H

Pte D'Andria, L P

Pte Davies, A

Pte Dennison, L – born Calverley, Yorks, no 2428: died of wounds 18 December 1915

Pte Docker, W

Pte Douglas, F

Pte Douglas, H

Pte Dowling, J

Pte Dyer, F

Pte Dyson, F S – no 2589: killed in action 25 July 1916

Pte Edmondson, P

Pte Evans, H

Pte Fairbank, A S

Pte Fairbank, F E – no 2044: awarded MM

Pte Featherstone, S – born Castleford, Yorks, no 2403: killed in action 3 September 1916

Pte Field, H W

Pte Field, J B

Pte Firth, J – born Horton, Yorks, no 1379: died 23 March 1916

Pte Foster, F L

Pte Foster, H – born Shipley, Yorks, no 1744: killed in action 19 November 1915

Pte Fox, W J – born Faversham, Kent, no 80030: killed in action 11 October 1918

Pte Garbutt, W

Pte Gawthorpe, A – no 3176: killed in action 1 July 1916

Pte Gellert, E – born Bradford, Yorks, no 235: killed in action 19 December 1915

Pte Gibson, G E

Pte Gill, A – born Bradford, Yorks, no 4564: killed in action 3 September 1916

Pte Gill, J – born Bradford, Yorks, no 1877: killed in action 24 September 1915

Pte Gillson, S

Pte Gough, P J

Pte Green, A

Pte Green, E

Pte Greensmith, G B

Pte Griffin, J

Pte Haigh, J W – born Meltham, Yorks, no 30753: killed in action 25 April 1918

Pte Hall, E

Pte Hall, L

Pte Hampshire, R

Pte Harrison, J W

Pte Harrison, L

Pte Healey, H

Pte Helliwell, R – born West Bowling, Yorks, no 1158: killed in action July 1916

Pte Henderson, H

Pte Hill, P A

Pte Hindley, H

Pte Hodgson, G K

Pte Hodgson, J J

Pte Holdsworth, C

Pte Hollings, W

Pte Holloway, F G

Pte Holmes, F

Pte Holmes, R H – born Horton, Yorks, no 422: killed in action 26 September 1916

Pte Horseman, S J

Pte Howlett, T E – born Bradford, Yorks, no 185: killed in action 27 September 1915

Pte Howitt, A

Pte Humphries, T

Pte Jackson, V – born Leeds, Yorks, no 240182: killed in action 3rd September 1916

Pte Jefferson, F

Pte Jennings, G T

Pte Jennings, J C

Pte Jones, C

Pte Keighley, P – no 2469: died of wounds 24 December 1915

Pte Kenefick, T E

Pte Kennedy, J T

Pte Kellett, G – born Bradford, Yorks, no 240291: killed in action 9 October 1917

Pte King, F

Pte Lawrence, J

Pte Lister, J – born Bradford, Yorks, no 1429: killed in action 11 August 1915

Pte Long, H – born Bradford, Yorks, no 240306: died of wounds 29 December 1917

Pte Lonsdale, G

Pte Lord, A C

Pte Lumby, S H – no 240612: killed in action 25 April 1918

Pte Lustig, H

Pte Maltby A E

Pte Margerison, A – born Thornbury, Yorks, no 2437: died of wounds 17 July 1915

Pte Marsden, W

Pte Martin, H

Pte Massey, P

Pte Matthewman, F – born Bramley, Yorks, no 1217: killed in action 21 July 1915

Pte Maufe, C G – died 3 February 1919

Pte McDonnell, G

Pte McPhail, W – born Bradford, Yorks, no 1689: killed in action 6 October 1915

Pte Mee, R

Pte Melhuish, H

Pte Metcalfe, W – born Saddleworth, Lancs, no 306613: killed in action 25 April 1918

Pte Miller, G H

Pte Mills, J

Pte Milnes, E

Pte Mitchell, G O

Pte Moore, A – born Bangor, Co Down, no 1630: killed in action 1 July 1916

Pte Morton, C

Pte Mossop, V

Pte Myers, W

Pte Narey, B P – died 4 February 1919

Pte New, D W

Pte Newby, C A – born Bradford, Yorks, no 2505: killed in action 19 August 1915

Pte Nightingale, A – born Southport, Lancs, no 2373: killed in action 19 December 1915

Pte Parker, G – born Shipley, Yorks, no 2344: killed in action 5 September 1915

Pte Parsey, N E

Pte Parsey, R

Pte Parsey, W R

Pte Pattinson, S

Pte Poole, G R – born Leeds, Yorks, no 72286: died of wounds 29 January 1917

Pte Rhodes, F W

Pte Rhodes, J A

Pte Riley, M W

Pte Robinson, A

Pte Robinson, C – no 3127: killed in action 19 November 1915

Pte Roome, F

Pte Ruddock, A

Pte Ruffe, E

Pte Scaife, G

Pte Schofield, C – born Bradford, Yorks, no 240478: died 31 October 1918

Pte Schofield, W – no 24184: died 1 August 1918

Pte Sellers, G N

Pte Simpson, G V

Pte Slimming, G

Pte Smith, A – born Windhill, Yorks, no 2108: killed in action 3 June 1915

Pte Smith, E

Pte Smith, G H

Pte Smith, H – no 2287: killed in action 12 October 1915

Pte Smith, H – no 54194: died of wounds 15 October 1918

Pte Stanley, J L

Pte Storrs, J

Pte Sykes, S W – born Manchester, Lancs, no 62975: killed in action 11 October 1918

Pte Taylor, W

Pte Terry, W

Pte Thackeray, E A

Pte Todd, J

Pte Tomlinson, J – born Bradford, Yorks, no 1593: killed in action 3 September 1916

Pte Townson, A J

Pte Turner, A

Pte Turpin, N – born Bradford, Yorks, no 211: killed in action 1 July 1916

Pte Unna, H G

Pte Unwin, W

Pte Vitty, E

Pte Waterhouse, D W – no 24115: died 23 October 1918

Pte Watkins, W – born Shipley, Yorks, no 1374: killed in action 29 August 1915

Pte Webb, W

Pte Westerman, H

Pte Whitaker, J C – no 241300: died of wounds 8 October 1917

Pte Whitaker, F W

Pte Willcock, H E – no 1360: awarded DCM

Pte Wilkinson, J E – born Bradford, Yorks, no 2449: died of wounds 17 November 1915

Pte Wilson, A

Pte Wilson, V

Pte Woddiwiss, B – no 240787: awarded MM

Pte Woolham, H – no 240737: awarded MM

Pte Wright, H R

Pte Wright, J

Captain E V Tempest's history of the battalion does not identify which commissioned officers (that is, 2nd Lt and above) were assigned specifically to 'C' Company. This second list therefore consists of all the battalion's commissioned officers who sailed for France on 15 April 1915, with their ranks shown on that date.

Where an officer is known to have been wounded, killed in action or to have died on active service, this is indicated. The gallantry medals are DSO, Distinguished Service Order, and MC, Military Cross.

Lt Col Wade, H O – awarded DSO: wounded 1 July 1916

Maj Scott, C E – wounded 28 July 1916: died of wounds 9 August 1916

Maj Clough, R – awarded MC: wounded 4 July 1916 and 11 October 1918

Capt Sandeman, G R – awarded MC

Capt Hill, W H – awarded MC

Capt Anderton, H L – wounded 7 February 1916 and 9 October 1917

Capt Fawcett, R A – wounded 1 July 1916

Capt Walker, A C C

Capt Barker, H W – wounded 3 November 1917

Capt Middleton, L S – wounded 15 December 1915

Capt Muller, J – awarded DSO and MC

Capt Muller, N – killed in action 28 July 1918

Capt Fell, R G

Lt Gordon, S J – awarded MC

Lt Hamilton, A – wounded 1 July 1916

Lt Heselton, J L – awarded DSO: wounded 1 July 1916

Lt Oddy, J L – wounded 1 July 1916: died of wounds 3 September 1916

Lt Tetley, W G – wounded 11 October 1915 and 14 August 1916

Lt Knowles, E W – wounded 25 September 1915 and 24 July 1916

Lt Musgrave, F W

Lt Grice, N – wounded 25 August 1915, 1 July 1916 and 19 November 1917

Lt Savill, S C – wounded 19 May 1915 and 11 May 1917

2nd Lt Dobson, R G – died 14 January 1919

2nd Lt McLaren, J M

2nd Lt Fawcett, W L – awarded MC

2nd Lt Hornshaw, F G – awarded MC

2nd Lt Armistead, T E – awarded MC: wounded 26 October 1916: killed in action 3 May 1917

2nd Lt Mossop, W N – awarded MC: wounded 12 August 1915: died of wounds 8 May 1918

2nd Lt Watson, J C

2nd Lt Myers, E – awarded MC: wounded 26 July 1915, 1 July 1916 and 4 August 1917

2nd Lt Birch, W L – awarded DSO: wounded 29 November 1915

Daily Timetable (Infantry)

THE DAILY TIMETABLE SET OUT BELOW was written by G.O.M. in the back of his copy of 1/6th Bn West Yorkshire Regiment Standing Orders. It is reproduced here to give an idea of what the pattern of life was like either at a quiet period in the front line or in the reserve trenches.

1. Stand to arms ½hr before daylight
   When satisfied all is clear, post day sentries
2. 7–8 am. Clean rifles and clean up trenches
3. 8–8.30 am. Breakfast
4. 8.30–12 Noon. Men who have not been at work at night told off to work where it is safe. Inspection of lines.
5. 12–1 pm. Dinner
6. 1–4.30 pm. Rest.
7. 4.30–5 pm. Tea.
8. 5 pm. Rifle inspection.
9. ½hr before dusk, stand to, inspection of firing positions. Night sentries posted.
10. (a) Night patrols, night listening parties and night working parties told off. The period of work follows after sentry duty. Sentries 1 in 10 by day, 1 in 3 by night. Officers and NCOs work by watches by night. Cooking done by platoons. *Latrine system receptacle* (buckets).
    (b) In addition to (a) above, snipers are told off.

Acknowledgements

This book started out as something else. I had intended the first chapter in a memoir of my own life to be about the experiences of my father, George Oswald Mitchell (G.O.M.), during the First World War. However, the more I explored the context in which he wrote his trench diary and notes, the more it became clear that a dozen or so pages would not do justice to the four and more years that he spent serving his country.

In attempting to convey the reality of his life on the Western Front, I have been greatly helped by a number of people and institutions. The Royal Engineers Archives and Library at Chatham allowed me access to and permission to quote from the *Special Brigade Newsletters* and from Martin S ('Syd') Fox's memoir *With the Special Brigade RE*, as well as permission to reproduce photographs showing aspects of gas warfare. I am also grateful to the Imperial War Museum Photographic Archive for allowing me to use a number of photographs from their remarkable collection.

I would have liked to be able to thank the Department of Documents at the Imperial War Museum, but cannot bring myself to do so. After my father died in January 1969, I presented his trench diary and his copy of 1/6th Bn West Yorkshire Regiment Standing Orders and Instructions to the Department of Documents at the Imperial War Museum, along with a number of photographs of him in uniform and documents relating to his war service, including his commission as a 2nd Lt. To my dismay, the Department of Documents has lost all the accompanying photographs and documents relating to G.O.M. I suppose I should be grateful that they have not lost his diary.

I am grateful to Palgrave Macmillan for permission to reproduce extracts from Harold Macmillan's *Winds of Change* (Macmillan & Co Ltd 1966).

Every effort has been made to contact or trace all copyright holders. The publishers would be glad to put right any omissions or errors brought to their notice at the earliest opportunity.

It would not have been possible for me to complete this book without Janet Powney's constant encouragement and help: her

comments on the draft text all focused on simplification and the banishment of obscurity. Michael Greenebaum and Christine Humphries also made helpful suggestions on some chapters. Veronica Mitchell, Dominic Mitchell and Alcuin Mitchell gave advice and provided support at critical stages.